Pets and the Afterlife 2

Rob Gutro

Pets and the Afterlife 2: Stories of signs from pets that passed

Cover

Cover Art: Created by Got You Covered @Covers by Lisa. https://www.facebook.com/CoversByLisa/, lisak39@aol.com

"Pets and the Afterlife 2," by Rob Gutro. ISBN-13: 978-1523799817 and ISBN-10: 1523799811

Dedication

This book dedicated to my mother, Norma, who passed from this life on December 29, 2013. She loved dogs, especially her beloved poodle and cocker spaniel. Both of her dogs were waiting for her on the other side; one even paid her a visit while she lay in a coma during her final days.

The experiences in this book are true. Some names have been changed to protect the privacy of the individual providing the story at their request.

I wish to acknowledge our dogs in spirit: Sprite and Buzz Wyatt, whose demonstration of unconditional love provided the inspiration for this book and the impetus for me to help those left behind to cope with their grief.

I wrote this book to help pet owners in their time of grief over the loss of their beloved pets. The physical form of our pets in this life is inconsequential. Pets of all types are members of our family, and dealing with their loss is very real and a significant life event.

My deepest appreciation to all who work with animal rescues, in kennels, shelters, and in veterinary medicine for the unconditional love they give to these wonderful animals.

Contents

PART 3: PET MESSAGES TO THEIR PARENTS

Foreword

Welcome to the second volume of "Pets and the Afterlife." If you are reading this book, you have most likely suffered the loss of a pet, and I want you to know that I am truly sorry for your loss. You need not read "Pets" 1 before reading this book. They stand on their own.

After reading this book, my hope is that you will come to realize that our departed pets are still with us. They can hear our words and our thoughts, even though they may not be with us in the physical plane.

***One important note:* I am not a grief counselor; I am a medium.** This book will not coach you on how to work through grief *(Read Pets 3 for coping with grief).* However, it is my hope that by learning how to recognize signs from your loved ones in spirit, it will help you work through that grief.

It's okay to be a skeptic, but I ask that you keep an open mind as you read this book. We all have a lot to learn about this life and the next. Many of the occurrences that we may be quick to dismiss may actually be a sign from Spirit that someone is attempting to communicate with us. Learning to communicate with Spirit begins with the understanding that there is no such thing as a coincidence. However, believing that everything may be a sign from a deceased loved one or pet is the other extreme; not everything is a sign from Spirit. I wrote this book so that you will begin to learn the ability to discern what may be a message of love for you.

This book builds off the first volume of "Pets and the Afterlife," as I have been developing my abilities to tune into pets on the other side who want to pass on messages. In this book, you will learn the who, what, when, where, why, and how our pets' spirits can give us signs.

Many of the experiences you will read about in this book are my own; others have been shared with the gracious permission of the grieving pet parents to demonstrate how their pets have communicated with them from the afterlife.

I do provide short e-mail readings for your pet in spirit. Details are on my website. For comprehensive human spirit readings, I recommend Ruthie Larkin, the Beantown Medium at www.Beantownmedium.com. I am also available for lectures, animal rescue fundraisers and speaking engagements. If interested, please contact me through email or my blog.

If you have questions or stories you would like to share, please write to me at Rgutro@gmail.com or through:

Amazon Author Page: https://tinyurl.com/vzy7kre

Blog: www.robgutro.com, www.petspirits.com
http://ghostsandspiritsinsights.blogspot.com/

Facebook:
https://www.facebook.com/RobGutroAuthorMedium or
https://www.facebook.com/ghostsandspirits.insightsfromamedium

Instagram: http://instagram.com/robgutro_author

Linked In: https://www.linkedin.com/in/rob-gutro-531a311b5/

Twitter: https://twitter.com/RobGutroAuthor

YouTube: https://tinyurl.com/wcvhqbt

I look forward to hearing from you and wish you peace and comfort knowing that our pets' love binds us to them "fur-ever."

Rob Gutro

Introduction

This book is comprised of three parts.

The first part includes a discussion on the intelligence of pets, and explains the basics about what happens to our pets after they pass, and the fundamental differences between a ghost and a spirit.

The second part includes messages that I have received from deceased pets who wanted to communicate with their "pet parents." After reading these stories, I think that you will agree that the intimate details these pets in Spirit were able to convey are truly amazing.

The third part includes personal stories from people who agreed to share their experiences. Each of these encounters holds a special place in their hearts, and provides evidence of the many diverse ways that pets in Spirit can communicate.

After reading this book, you will be better equipped to know what signs to look for from your own pets, and be able to recognize their attempts to communicate with you.

My Lifetime Experiences with Dogs
I grew up in a family that owned dogs. Today, my husband and I are the proud "dog parents" to two Dachshunds and a Weimaraner. We have been working with dog rescues since 2009 and do transports, fostering, home visits, assist with website work, promotions, events and fundraising.

We learn a lot from our pets, and by far, their gift of unconditional love is the greatest lesson of them all.

My experience with dogs began as a young child. When I was growing up in the 1960s and 1970s, dogs were not typically as well-treated as they are today. That is, unless we're talking about my Italian mother. She loved our family dogs with all of her heart and she even made them clothing for the winter long before it was even thought of commercially. In fact, I still have all of the sweaters and coats she made for her Poodle, and use them in winter as they fit our Dachshunds. I half-joke that my mother loved her dogs more than she loved her three boys, however, there's some truth to that!

Our first family dog was a copper-colored Cocker Spaniel named "Penny." I believe that Penny laid the foundation for my lifelong affinity for dogs. My mother said that Penny was well-behaved and very easy going. My memories of Penny are few, consisting of only mental images of her walking around in my parents' house, and this one.

I was just four years old in 1967. My mother was talking on the phone that hung on the wall in our kitchen. Dad had taken

Penny to the vet earlier that day, and my mother listened quietly to the prognosis. She slowly sank down to sit on the bench. Penny would not be coming home. My mother hung up the phone and wept uncontrollably. One of the earliest memories I can recall is the loss of our family's beloved pet. So many of us have memories just like this, which is why I offer hope and evidence that our pets in the afterlife are capable of communicating with us.

I've also read studies that indicate that we grieve more deeply for the loss of a pet than we do for other humans. Of course, while you're thinking about that statement a few of those humans may come to mind!

Dogs and cats hold a special place in my life and my heart as I am sure they have one in yours if you are reading this book. Just know that they will always have a place in your heart, and they will always be part of you as you will always be part of them.

###

Part I:
How Pets Can and Do Communicate from Spirit

Chapter 1
What Happens After a Pet Passes?

Dealing with the death of a pet is traumatic. To many of us, it's like losing a family member. After we acknowledge a pet's physical passing, some of us worry that we may never see them again. I assure you that you will see them again, and know that our relatives and friends have also passed are anxiously waiting for them on the other side, calling to them, and assisting them to cross over.

When your pet passes, you can request that someone you know in spirit be there to help your dog or cat cross over. Spirits on the other side hear us. In my first "Pets and the Afterlife" book, I tell the story of when I asked my dad and a friend, Ed, to be there waiting for our dachshund, Sprite, when it was his time to pass. The day after Sprite's passing, both my dad and Ed confirmed for me that Sprite was indeed with them when each sent pennies marked with the year or their passing. You'll learn that when it comes to Spirit, there's no such thing as a coincidence.

Before we learn how our pets are able to communicate with us as a ghost or spirit, it's important to provide an explanation of how physical death and the afterlife works with humans that are in Spirit, because they are remarkably similar. It's also important to learn what a soul really is, and why some people question whether or not pets have souls (of course they do).

Soul 101: What is a Soul?
All living things have a "soul." Every human and animal has a "soul" and a consciousness. Even plants have awareness as science has documented that they "scream" when being cut or killed. The collective energies of every living thing can be considered a part of the "god energy" or an energy source of light.

3

At the point of physical death, the energy that propels an Earth-bound body combines with the soul – memories and personality of the living being (whether human or animal) – and does one of two things: departs this Earthly plane and joins the multitude of other energies that run through the universe as a "spirit," or stays here on Earth as a "ghost."

After a couple of recent radio interviews, it occurred to me that some people really don't have a good idea about what a "soul" really is, and if they are limited to humans (for some reason). In many societies and religions a soul is the immortal essence of a living thing. A soul is actually the energy in every living thing that combines memories and personalities.

Of course animals have souls. Every living thing has a soul. To think otherwise is nonsensical. Animals (and dinosaurs) lived and died on Earth long before humans ever showed up. They survived because they had intelligence, instinct, emotions, memories, and their own personalities.

After all, what makes one animal a pack leader and not all of them? Why are some animals shy? Why are some animals easily frightened, while others are bold? That's personality. They all have it, just as humans do.

Do Animals Have Souls?
Most Abrahamic religions espouse that only human beings possess an immortal soul; Evangelical-Biblical literalists fall squarely into this category. In 2015, in marked contrast to their Protestant counterparts, the Catholic Church issued a cautiously worded statement clarifying their position that animals and plants do have souls, but lack conceptual intelligence. A position that is equally ridiculous. Any living thing that develops the survival instinct possesses both intelligence and a soul.

Some religions do believe that animals have souls. Sikhism, Hinduism and Orthodox believe and understand that animals have souls.

Rest assure that the departure of a soul at the moment of physical death is identical in both humans and animals. A soul may choose to stay Earthbound as a ghost or cross over as a spirit. *A spirit is a spirit.* Period. *Only zombies are soul-less.*

Spirits

In the afterlife, energies that have joined the collective "Spirit" (all of the spirits) have successfully made the transition to the next plane of existence; some refer to this next plane as Heaven, Valhalla, Zion, Paradise or Nirvana.

Spirits do not linger on Earth. Spirits of people and animals have the ability to return to Earth from time to time to pass messages to the living. Spirits also learn on the other side. They learn how to communicate better, they also link up with other spirits that they knew on the Earthly plane, or knew previously in spirit.

Ghosts

Ghosts on the other hand are energies that have not left this Earthly plane. A ghost may choose to be Earth-bound for reasons that may include the following: their death was either sudden, like an accident or caused by some violent means; they lack the understanding that their physical body has ceased to function; or perhaps there is some matter of unresolved business that may involve revenge or the need to obtain forgiveness from someone who is still living. Occasionally, some pets will stay behind as ghosts if they don't get help from our relatives on the other side (although they usually do).

A pet may choose to stay behind as an Earth-bound ghost so that they will stay with their pet parent until the parent also passes. That doesn't happen often, but it can happen. Mostly, though, our pets cross over as our friends and relatives are there to welcome them.

Although ghosts may be aware of the other energies that have joined Spirit, it is my belief that they are unable to communicate with them across the divide that separates the two realms. If they could, then our late relatives would quickly bring any pets into the light who have either ignored them or chosen to remain earthbound.

Two Types of Earth-bound Hauntings

There are two types of hauntings associated with Earth-bound ghosts: "intelligent hauntings" and "residual hauntings." Ghosts participating in an intelligent haunting are capable of independent thought and possess the ability to directly communicate and interact with the living.

Characteristics of an intelligent haunting include objects moving independently of their own accord, noise generation (e.g., footsteps, disembodied voices, EVPs), or even physical manifestations such as full body apparitions. Keep in mind that the apparitions require a substantial amount of energy and are usually indicative of an extremely powerful presence. Residual hauntings are not interactive, but rather the "thumbprint" of emotional energy that has been left behind.

Residual hauntings are characterized by repeated actions or scenes, and can be likened to watching a movie that keeps playing the same scene over and over again, as in a perpetual loop. Ghosts participating in a residual haunting do not possess independent thought, and are incapable of communicating with the living.

Using Energy to Communicate

Both ghosts and spirits, however, use energy – both physical and emotional energy – as the conduit to help in their communication with us. Entities that possess very low energy levels are capable

6

of tapping the physical energy from an alternative source, e.g., heat, light, moving water, in an effort to boost their energy levels so they can break through the membrane barrier that separate our two existences to communicate with us.

Emotional energy works in a similar manner as physical energy. A group of people gathered together (e.g., a prayer meeting in a church, a funeral or wake, a wedding or birthday party) can collectively raise the emotional energy level and can easily be tapped by an entity.

Emotional energy can be either negative or positive. Earthbound ghosts however, only energize from negative emotional energy, while spirits become empowered by positive emotional energy. Examples of negative emotional energy include fear, anxiety, nervousness, anger and hatred. On the other hand, examples of positive emotional energy includes love, optimism, faith, hope, and happiness. It is important that we provide the right type of emotional energy – preferably position – when we wish to receive a message from Spirit.

Good, Good, Good Vibrations
Both spirits and ghosts are at a higher vibrational plane than we are in the physical world. So in order for a spirit to communicate with the living, they must lower the level of their vibrations. It sounds like science fiction, but it's not. Think about the electromagnetic spectrum. Light is a vibration. The entire spectrum of visible light produces different colors. You can see them when you shine a light through a prism or look at a rainbow. Ultraviolet light is the highest frequency and shortest wavelength, and infrared light is the lowest frequency and longest wavelength.

There are other kinds of vibrations as well. Emotions are a type of vibration. Feeling good generates a high vibration and that's where spirits are. Conversely, feeling poor generates a low vibration. Sound is another type of vibration. Soothing music or music that enhances mood is a high vibration, while loud or irritating music gives off a lower vibration.

When spirits are trying to communicate they must match the vibrations of the physical world to come through to us. The point here is that it's easier for a spirit to get through to you with messages when you are at a higher vibration. That's why if you are still struggling with grief from the loss of your pet, you are at a lower vibration and harder for spirit to reach. Being at a lower vibration requires a spirit to use much more energy to break through to you.

A Pet's Love is Energy

Our pets are a living embodiment of unconditional love. They, like people, possess the same type of energy as humans. When they pass, their energy has the same choice to make in the afterlife as humans – to either join the collective universe, or remain Earth-bound as a ghost.

Anyone that tells you that our pets do not have a soul is quite simply uninformed. Our pets are waiting to greet us when it is our time to pass. It is not unusual for the ghosts and spirits of pets to linger near their masters. I have seen them, as have many other mediums. Wouldn't the world be a better place if only people would learn to love unconditionally?

##

Chapter 2
How Do Pet Spirits Communicate to the Living?

This chapter is likely to be one of the most important chapters you'll read because it explains some of the more common ways that pets and people in spirit attempt to communicate with us from the other side. You'll want to read this chapter several times so that you won't miss any!

How Do Pets Give Signs?

As with humans, pets tend to give us signs around the anniversaries of significant events and holidays. Some examples of a significant event in the life of a pet would include the date when they were adopted, the date of when the passed, or the date when their birthday was celebrated. Attempts to communicate are not strictly limited to those times, but attempts to communicate are heightened, and we are most likely feeling the need to hear from someone during these times.

Reflect for a moment on how we communicate with a human relative that lives a significant distance away from us. We may call or email them on birthdays, anniversaries, holidays or special occasions. Well it's no different when people or pets are in Spirit. They want to communicate with you at those times and they can do it in number of ways.

Before I get into how they can give signs, it's important to understand that time doesn't matter on the other side, so spirits can give us messages six days or sixty years after they pass. Time only matters in the physical plane.

There are many ways that you can get signs from loved ones in spirit, and they are really unlimited. The signs that spirit can provide are usually associated with something they may have known when alive in the physical plane, or something that you would identify with.

Music is one way spirits let us know they're still connected and still with us from time to time. A friend of mine heard her and her late husband's song "Good Morning, Star-shine" on the radio on the date of what would've been their 42nd anniversary. The day that my dog Buzz passed I walked into the house and heard Garth Brooks' song "The Dance" about a man who was grateful for the limited time he had with someone he loved. That was the first sign I received from Buzz.

A musical sign from spirit also includes hearing a song that was the person's favorite, and that you may rarely hear. In the case of Buzz's first sign, "The Dance" was 15 years old and not aired much on the radio. The song could also be heard from someone else's car that you "just happened" (read: were guided by spirit) to drive up next to in traffic. Or as in the case of a message from my mom, one of her favorite songs "Everywhere" by Fleetwood Mac was playing when I walked into a CVS to get a greeting card (and I accidentally picked up a card with a poodle on it - which was also her favorite breed of dog). There are no coincidences with Spirit.

Manipulation of things or even life forms in nature is also a way that spirits send us signs. The sudden appearance of birds, butterflies, or perhaps other insects are all likely attempts to communicate from the other side. For example, if after someone passes and a bird starts showing up at your bedroom window each morning for a couple of days, it may be a sign from Spirit.

Spirits (and ghosts) can also allow you to hear their voice (e.g., as in a bark or a meow). You may also hear their collar jingle, or hear their favorite toy squeak, or mysteriously fall from a shelf.
You may see a passing shadow in your peripheral vision, or actually see the manifestation of a person or pet in full color as I did with my dog Buzz after he passed. Several cat parents have reported to me

that they have seen a shadow dart along the floor, just as their cat had done in life, scoot from room to room when in the physical.

Spirits and ghosts will also share odors that would identify them to you, whether it be the smell of a dog's fur, or a woman's perfume or cigar smoke.

You could find coins, especially with a date that is relevant to them. Spirits often move coins to let us know they're around because it doesn't take as much energy to move something so small. The movement of something from one place to another by supernatural means is called an apport. Spirits use this ability all the time.

Finding a flower that reminds you of them or seeing something in clouds, are other ways spirits let you know they're about.

Spirits will also lead us to someone that looks like them on a certain day, to remind us they are still connected. The trick is being aware of everything around you so you don't miss something!

They can also manipulate anything electronic! Remember, ghosts and spirits are all energy, so it makes it easy to manipulate energy. They can turn your television or radio on and off, or flash the lights in the house. Sometimes, spirits, usually human spirits, will make your phone ring and no one will be on the other side. However, sometimes people have reported hearing the voice of their late loved one on the other end of the phone (usually through static).

Watch for signs from your pets and people. They send them. We just have to be open-minded and pay attention.

How Do I Get Messages?
The first question people ask me is, "Do you see dead people and pets?" The answer to that is yes and no.

I don't see ghosts and spirits in physical form like they're standing in an elevator with me, but I do "see" what they look like using my mind's eye. It's like telepathy. In fact, sometimes I see them so clearly that I am able to sketch them in a notebook that I carry with me on paranormal investigations. Even after doing this for several years, it's still a bit unnerving to me when a client is able to identify the entity in a drawing that I have created in this manner.

In addition to "seeing" spirits, I am also able to hear them. I hear words or snippets of words, names, dates, and sentences. Some tell me why they are there, what they're doing, or what they want. Others tell me if they don't want to be bothered or if they have an urgent message.

I've felt spirits, felt their emotions, smelled their scents, and seen them in dreams. I have also been able to feel their physical pain at the moment of death, or have them relate to me how they passed.

In one instance I had just started talking with a woman at a dog rescue fundraiser and she said that her dog passed. I immediately heard "poison" and asked her if the dog was poisoned. She was shocked. She asked how I knew that. I told her that I heard the word and it came from the spirit of her dog who was right there with us. Of course, it was the confirmation she needed that her beloved dog was still around her in spirit.

Dogs, cats, horses, and some birds can provide these signs. Most often, though, they'll use pictures. They'll show me something they were familiar with in their physical life to prove their identity to the pet parent.

The first several chapters of this book contains all of these ways that pets have communicated through me.

My Beginnings as a Medium

Since I was a teenager I have had the ability to see, sense, and communicate with those who have passed from the physical world.

My grandfather appeared to me as a full-body, full- color apparition in July 1976, six months after he died. I came to realize that July also marked his birthday month, and spirits usually come back on birthdays, anniversaries and holidays, so it made sense he came to me when he did.

For many decades I ignored my inherited abilities and never paid attention to them because I lacked the understanding of how to fully use them, and I didn't have the emotional and spiritual maturity to develop them.

As my life started coming together, I fell in love, married, and settled into a reasonably comfortable life with my partner. It was about this time that my abilities began to increase exponentially and became too intense to ignore. The time was right to learn more about this gift that I had received; specifically how to develop the ability to communicate with those who have passed.

I joined the paranormal investigation group Inspired Ghost Tracking in 2010, and have used my abilities to solve mysteries of haunted locations. I've been in many private residences and historic buildings, where I've received messages, discovered the identities of the Earth-bound ghost and helped cross them over.

As my ability has developed, I have learned that being able to communicate with those in the afterlife is not just limited to communication with humans, but also with animals. I will provide evidence of this later, but I ask that as you read this book, keep an open mind to the things you may not immediately understand; realize that our souls are living energy and that we are all connected both here in the physical realm and in the spiritual realm.

I have written several books about my experiences as a way to provide comfort and hope to those left behind; my aim for the books was to help others see that our loved ones who have passed are still with us and come to visit from time to time.

##

Chapter 3
Pets Are More Intelligent Than We Think

Whenever I give a talk about how pets are able to communicate I begin by telling the audience that the manner in which we treat our pets is comparatively similar to how we treat human children.

Consider the following: We teach them words so they understand our language. We are excited when they share their toys and play well with others. We encourage them to exercise, eat right, and take naps. We play with them, cuddle them, sometimes buy them clothing, or at least leashes, collars and beds.

We are excited when they learn how to go to the bathroom (outside in the case of a dog, in a litter box for a cat, and a toilet for a human child). We take them to school for obedience training or agility, or something else. Some pet parents show their pets off in pageants or kennel shows just as parents watch their human children in talent shows.

I tell people that the basic difference between a human child and a pet, other than possessing the ability to communicate on a high level, is that our pets don't grow up, leave the house, start a career, and marry someone you may dislike!

Pets Possess Emotions
In my first "Pets and the Afterlife," I cited scientific studies performed by Dr. Gregory Berns of Emory University who analyzed the emotional reactions in a dog's brain by scanning and recording their responses using MRIs. He determined that the caudate of a dog's brain reacts exactly the same was as a human's when showing different emotions. He wrote about his studies in a wonderful book called *How Dogs Love Us: A Neuroscientist and His Adopted Dog Decode the Canine Brain.*

Pets are capable of understanding us on an emotional level and even possess the ability to show emotions themselves. Dogs experience all kinds of emotion from joy to depression to grief. Think about this: whenever we're sad or sick our pets come to us to offer comfort and succor. When they themselves feel that way, they either seek extra attention from us or wish to be left alone. Think on the patterns and behaviors of people in your own life. Do they want to be alone when sick or depressed? Do they wish to be surrounded by people to comfort them?

Pets possess the ability to grieve in a similar manner as humans. If a dog has a companion, and the companion passes away, you will notice the surviving dog acting differently. Perhaps the surviving dog does not want to play, or eat or does something the dog who passed used to do. If you have two pets and one passes, you will notice the other may become lethargic, seem depressed, and even keep searching for the other pet.

The night after my puppy Buzz was killed by a car in February 2005, my roommate's (at the time) Border Collie picked up and carried Buzz's stuffed toy badger around. He had never touched that toy previously in the months before. It was the Border Collie's way of telling me he was grieving over the loss of Buzz (I was walking him the same time as Buzz when the accident happened, so the Border Collie saw the entire accident, too).

You may notice, however, that if your dog is looking at what appears to be an empty corner and is wagging his tail, he is very likely looking at the spirit of the companion who passed and has come back for a visit. Dogs and cats have the ability to see spirits and ghosts because of a physiological difference in the makeup of their eyes.

The Research: Pets are Smart in So Many Ways

Now I'm going to focus on the intelligence of pets, because pets are intelligent enough to communicate with us from the other side after they've passed.

In the first volume of "Pets and the Afterlife" I discussed the different levels of learning development in dogs. Dr. Stanley Coren, DVM published several books describing in depth the characteristics of each level which include language and gestures, game playing, instinctual intelligence, emotional intelligence, loyalty, a daily routine, recognition of locations, different barks and body language, and facial signals. Dr. Coren's research showed that dogs possess the intelligence of a 2 to 4-year-old child.

Another researcher on the topic, Temple Grandin, likened the intelligence level in dogs to that of an autistic child. It was only by reading Temple Grandin's *Animals in Translation* that I was able to decipher what was scaring my Weimaraner, Dolly whenever I let her out in our fenced in backyard. After reading Grandin's book, I investigated the backyard in search of anything that could be identified as the source of Dolly's fear. My investigation revealed that an unstrapped silver-colored grill cover, caught in the wind, to be the culprit. After removing the grill cover, Dolly was no longer afraid of going outside; I just had to see the world as she saw it.

Another book that I found extremely helpful in understanding the intelligence of dogs is *The Genius of Dogs* by Brian Hare and Vanessa Woods. In their book, the authors summarize the incredible findings of scientific papers on dog cognition. Through science-based exercises, the authors demonstrate that dogs know how to reason, communicate, possess the ability to empathize, use cunning, and have phenomenal memories. They also explore a dog's cognitive abilities using existing knowledge to generate new knowledge. Dogs think and reason just like humans! For me, the book provided a fascinating synopsis of the link between domestication and intelligence.

The *Genius of Dogs* references how dogs follow visual clues whenever a human points. Wolves didn't follow that visual clue. Dogs will nudge you and sometimes bring something to you, like a ball if they want to play. They're clearly communicating with you about what they want to do.

The authors note that dogs have different barks, a trait that Dr. Coren also notes. There are barks of happiness, such as whenever my in-laws come for a visit. There are barks of alarm for whenever a person comes to the front door, and so on. Later I'll share a personal story of how our dogs' barking clued us in on the presence of my mother's spirit.

Dogs also have different growls. Just listen to your dog whenever they're in different situations. When our Weimaraner and youngest Dachshund play, the Weimaraner will growl, but it's a non-threatening "play growl." It sounds quite different from her protective threatening growl whenever someone approaches.

In addition to citing the results of scientific studies performed by others in the research community, Hare and Woods also describe the results of some very interesting studies they conducted. They noticed that dogs prefer working with people when they can see their eyes as opposed to being obscured by sunglasses or a blindfold. It made me think of how uncomfortable it makes me feel when I'm talking with someone who won't look me in the eye. Eye contact establishes a certain level of trust.

The authors' website "Dognition" provides a valuable resource tool to "evaluate cognition [and] provide a complete picture of your dog's intelligence and discovering which skills an individual dog relies on to navigate the world." Check out the Dognition website at www.dognition.com where you can learn more about your pet's thinking, learning, and problem-solving behavior through science-based games.

Seeing Those Qualities in Our Dogs

I have noticed all of these traits in our dogs. They can figure out how to get around obstacles without me telling them. They can lead each other to a toy or treat, or nudge one another away from a place they shouldn't be.

Our youngest Dachshund, Tyler, came to us as a rescue when he was 3 years old. He didn't know any words, including his own name; he wasn't housebroken; he didn't get along with other dogs, and he was just a terror. He marked in the house on purpose – a sign of defiance. Eventually, he formed a close bond with our Weimaraner, who taught him the ropes. He began to follow her everywhere and I watched him learn from her. It was amazing.

We took Tyler to obedience school and I continually used hand gestures to help train him. He clearly recognized the hand gestures and now I just have to point in the down direction, and he'll sit. All of our dogs were trained to recognize instructions using hand gestures, and know the same command if I speak it without the hand gesture. Basically, they can figure it out!

Tyler noticed that whenever we enter a room with a closed door that we would push the door open. So, he began, on his own, to push against the door with his nose to get inside. Even when we're not home, he will open the door to get up on his favorite piece of furniture. He reasoned that to get inside the room he wanted, he had to apply force to the door.

If you ever take your dog on a car ride, I'm sure you notice that they recognize landmarks, just as we do. Whenever we're about a mile from my in-laws' house, our dogs will start barking happily and wag their tails in anticipation. They know where they are just as we do. They know where they live. They know where friends live, the location of doggy day care, obedience school, dog parks, or friends' houses.

Pets have memories and a sense of direction as well, if not better than we do. In fact, we have to use GPS devices and they don't. I've read many stories in the news about dogs being lost hundreds of miles from home and walking back to their homes.

The bottom line is, since a dog has all of these abilities, they can certainly communicate with us as a spirit.

##

Chapter 4
Pets Know When It's Their Time

In the previous chapters I've talked about the intelligence of pets. That intelligence also includes a personal awareness of when their time in the physical plane is coming to an end.

Pets like people choose the timing of when they would like to pass; some will let you know that they want your help while others retreat to solitude. Like people who wait to pass until all of their loved ones are gathered around their death bed, some pets want to ensure they see all of their human and pet family members before they pass.

Pets will show their parents they don't want to go on by not eating, being lethargic, not responding to attention. Those are signs that prompt us to contact the vet to help them pass in peace.

Other times, a pet may retreat to a corner of the house and pass quietly. You'll read about both types of these responses in this book.

One of the most important lessons is that like people, pets choose when they want to pass and whether they want to be alone when it happens or be in the company of loved ones. It's a personal choice, just as it is for people.

All too often, pet parents have told me they feel guilt for not being there when their pets have passed. But there is no need to feel that guilt because our pet made the choice to pass when he or she did, either with or without their pet parents.

Our pets also do not want us to feel guilt for not helping them cross earlier. They will let us know when the time is right.

The following note came from Audrey, who shared the experience of her dog Quincy's passing. Quincy waited for his dad to come home before he passed and wanted to be with his dad when it was Quincy's time to move on. Audrey's story also hints that her dog Aspen saw her late dog, Quincy's spirit.

Audrey's Note about Quincy
Hi Rob, I am near the end of your book [Pets and the Afterlife]. Fascinating the way current pets communicate with passed pets.

My husband Steve had a strong relationship with [our dog] Quincy who passed away six years ago.

The first year we had [our dog] Aspen (five years ago), she could not be lured to the lower level of the house where Steve watches TV and where the laundry room is. After a year or so, she would come down briefly to check on me and then bolt back upstairs. She was clearly spooked. After a while, when she would venture down there briefly, she would always be looking around up high in the air at "nothing." Since the TV area downstairs is where Steve hangs out, I'm wondering if Quincy comes back to hang with Steve. Now Aspen doesn't mind being down there with us (though she would never go down there on her own).

I was also moved by your account of putting your 16 ½-year-old dog Sprite down. I had a similar, though opposite guilt with Quincy. At the end of his life, Quincy was suffering so much from cancer. On a Thursday morning he could barely stand to go out for his morning walk. I told Steve this couldn't go on and it was time. Steve called that day to make an appointment for Friday morning. That Thursday evening Quincy hung on until Steve came home. It was clearly his last moment and he was waiting to see Steve.

Steve picked him up and put in the car (his totally favorite place) and he died there on the way to the vet. He did spare Steve the difficulty of making a decision, but I felt, and still feel, that Quincy's last days were full of pain and I regretted not taking him to the vet sooner.

BTW, we have Quincy's ashes in a spare bedroom, but now I am going to put it downstairs in Steve's TV area.

Why Some Pets Show a Burst of Energy Before Passing

In 2015, during an interview I had with Darkness Radio, I was asked "Why do Pets show a Burst of Energy before putting them to sleep?"

Dave, the host said that he experienced that with his dogs before they were euthanized. My husband and I had a similar experience when we were driving our 16½-year-old dachshund, Sprite, to the vet for the event. Sprite's body was failing in so many ways. He hadn't eaten for a couple of days, but on the drive to the vet, he enthusiastically ate some Beggin' Strip treats.

So, why do dogs and cats get a "burst of energy" near the end sometimes? The answer is that the dog or cat knows you are helping them move out of pain and cross over into a pain free part of life, and they know that you're doing it out of the intense love you share.

So, although this burst of energy at the end causes grief in pet parents, our pets exhibit it because they're happy to cross over, and thankful pet parents love them enough to recognize that.

###

Chapter 5
Why Time Passed is Irrelevant

The concept of time does not exist on the other side. Spirits can give us messages sixty days or sixty years after they pass. Time is only relevant to us in the physical plane. In this chapter I'll explain all of the ways that my dog Buzz showed me that time doesn't matter on the other side with signs he provided more than a decade after his passing.

To understand why it doesn't matter if your beloved human or pet passed one month ago or ten years ago in terms of their ability to communicate with you, let's discuss the concept of time.

Here on Earth, we "age" based on the length of time it takes for the Earth to complete one orbit around the sun. So 365 days is equivalent to one year.

Time is all relative to where you are located. Put simply, think about the amount of time it takes for Jupiter to orbit the sun: once every 11.86 Earth years (or 4,332 days). That's because its 483.4 million miles (778 million kilometers) from the sun and Earth is about 93.2 million miles (150 million kilometers) from the sun. So, if humans lived on Jupiter, their average life span would be about 7 years or 83 Earth years old. For natives of Jupiter, Earthlings would appear to have very short lives. So, time is relative to your location.

Further, famous physicist Albert Einstein's theory of relativity found that space and time were interwoven into a single continuum known as space-time. Events that occur at the same time for one observer could occur at different times for another.

Buzz the Great Spirit Communicator

On February 22, 2005, my first dog, Buzz Wyatt, was struck and killed by a car. At that moment, time for me stood still.

Immediately after his passing, Buzz became the world's best canine communicator: from doppelgangers to moving objects, from a bark in the house to the sound of nails on the hardwood floor.

In one instance I followed what I thought was my newly adopted Weimaraner into the living room only to see no one there. So I ran upstairs to check on my newly adopted pup, Dolly, and found her fast asleep on my bed. At that moment I realized I had actually followed Buzz's spirit downstairs.

In the months after Buzz's passing, I would often hear two songs playing on the radio about losing the love of your life: Garth Brooks' song "The Dance," and Alan Jackson's "(My Heart is as Empty as a) Monday Morning Church." Over the years whenever I would think of Buzz, those songs would play on the radio or a CD or in a store. The former song came out in 1993, so it was odd to continue to hear it so many years later.

I've also found signs that he would send in the form of coins marked with the year "2005" - the year of his passing. When thinking of him or around the anniversary of his birthday, or date of his adoption or passing, I've seen butterflies or other things in nature that appeared out of place.

I wrote about all of those things and more in the previous volume of "Pets and the Afterlife." The book also contains chapters from three other mediums with their canine spirit communicators.

A Sign from Buzz a Decade Later

As I mentioned in Chapter 1, spirits come around on birthdays, anniversaries and holidays to let us know they're still around us.

Dogs and cats are no different from spirit people. They all acknowledge those events with us. In this case, I received a message on the anniversary of Buzz's passing.

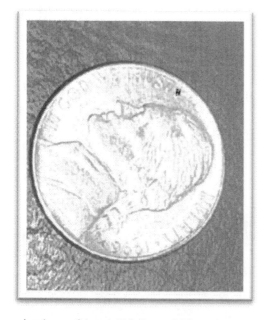

(Photo: Nickel from Ed. Credit: R. Gutro)

Ten years after Buzz passed in 2015, I received a sign from him with help from a human spirit of a friend named Ed who passed in 1996.

On the night of February 11, 2015 (almost 10 years to the day of his passing) I asked Buzz Wyatt to send me a sign that he's around. I also asked our friend Ed (in spirit) to let me know that Buzz is with him (he always wanted a dog in life and never adopted one). The next day, February 12, I got the answer.

At lunchtime I drove to the post office to mail a package and parked next to a curb. I got out of my truck and looked down and around (to make sure I wasn't too close to the curb) and there was nothing there. I mailed the package, and came back to the truck. As I was walking to the driver's side door, right next to it was a shiny nickel. When I saw it, I said in my head "Hello Edward!"

Spirits love to use coins to send messages they're around- and check the year, because if it means something to you or them- you'll have a better idea of who sent it. I didn't see the year until picked it up. It was dated 1996. 1996 was the year my friend Ed passed. It was from Ed, and I heard him in my head say that "I've got my other dog." Our dog Sprite passed on July 8, 2013, and Ed let us know he was with him at that time. Now, Ed confirmed that Buzz was there with him, too.

I was looking for a sign and I got it - from both Ed and Buzz working together.

A Physical Sign from Buzz on His 11th Birthday

Buzz was born on July 29, 2004, and he passed on February 22, 2005. During the week of his birthday in 2015, I received his sign through one of his photos we have hanging in the house.

The night before I realized it was a sign, I was the last one to go down the stairs (everyone else was in bed downstairs). Each night, as I walk down the stairs to go to bed, I look at Buzz's photo and those of our other late dog Sprite, my parents and our friend Ed's photos - all of which line the stairway and I say goodnight to all of them. I distinctly remember that all of the photos were horizontal.

Early the next morning I had to get something in my home office (it was before the dogs got upstairs). No one had gone up or down stairs between the time I descended the previous night to the time I ascended the stairs early the next morning, however, I noticed that out of all the photos on the wall, only Buzz's photo was at an extreme angle.

His photo is too high for any of our dogs to reach, and none of the other photos had been moved.

I realized that he was letting me know that 11 years later, he's still around (I sense him around anyway), but he wanted to provide physical proof.

28

(Photo: Buzz's spirit tipped his picture around his birthday. Credit: R. Gutro)

In the next section, you'll read about how other dogs and cats gave me detailed messages to confirm that they are still around their pet parents from time to time.

##

Chapter 6
Dogs React to Spirit Visits

Dogs and cats have the ability to see, hear, and sense earth-bound ghosts and spirits. They can do this because the can see faster motion than humans, can hear at higher frequencies than humans, and they rely on their feelings and instinct to sense things. Humans on the other hand discount entities because we try to explain them logically or reason them away.

Physiologically, dogs and cats are different than people because of the different configuration of cones and rods in their eyes. Cone cells can detect different colors while rods are for sensing motion and function best in low light. Both cones and rods receive light in the retina.

That difference between dogs and cats and humans is that they see movement that occurs at higher vibrations (covered in Chapter 1). In Pets and the Afterlife 1, I explained more about how their eyes perceive the world differently than the one humans see.

In terms of their hearing, dogs hear at higher frequencies than humans, which is very likely that range where ghosts and spirits "talk." Usually, people can't hear a spirit unless they spirit has a lot of energy. You'll read about some strong pet spirits later that were able to bark or meow after they passed, and loud enough to be heard by humans!

Normally, though, humans can't hear ghosts or spirits speak at the higher frequency, so paranormal investigators use digital recorders to pick up their voices.

My Dogs React to My Mother's Electrical Manipulation

On Monday, April 6, 2015, I was teleworking when my mom's spirit paid a visit, and made her presence known by manipulating electricity! Fortunately, I had the wherewithal to record and try to debunk this manifestation in the 30 seconds it was happening.

Around 3 p.m. EDT I was working from home on our sun porch. Our three dogs, who had been quietly sleeping, were suddenly awakened and started to bark. I didn't hear anything, but I soon had a headache in the back of my head, my telltale sign indicating the presence of an entity.

I immediately got up from my chair and went into the kitchen and observed each light bulb in the chandelier over our kitchen table turning bright and then dimming all by itself! I sensed that the entity was the spirit of a woman. I whipped out my cell phone and recorded the phenomenon with the chandelier, and then walked over to the switch and tapped on the switch to show that switch was in the "OFF" position.

Because spirits are energy, they possess the ability to manipulate electricity, and make lights go dim or bright. They can also manipulate televisions, radios, cell phones, or other electronic devices. Spirits of pets, like humans, can also "play" with anything electric.

I acknowledged the spirit, but because the dogs also saw her they would not stop barking. They had known my mom in the physical sense, and obviously they recognized her because it was a happy bark, not an irritated bark.

To see the video of my mother's spirit playing with the lights in our kitchen, go to https://youtu.be/_9RH6_SqGgo

In "Pets and the Afterlife" book one, I relayed a story about a poodle who barked when he saw his dad's spirit leave his body as he passed. The following story was sent to me after Connie read that story.

Barking at her Husband's Spirit
Connie said: *When I lost my husband, my dog would always look down the hallway and bark...if they can make contact while alive I know they can after death.*

***

So if your dog or cat is staring at what appears to be nothing, it very well may be a spirit or a ghost (more likely a spirit because many houses are not haunted). If you think you know who the spirit may be, it is perfectly acceptable to address the spirit. Tell the spirit that you know they're there. If you think they're disturbing your pets, ask them politely to leave. If not, welcome them!

##

Chapter 7
Dreaming/Visits of Dogs (and Cats)

In a later chapter, you will read about a dream or visit from the spirit of a dog who saved her dad's life by reviving him after he blacked out during a serious condition.

Dreams are the easiest way in which our spirit pets and people can communicate. That's because our logical minds are asleep. Both our grief and our logical mind prevent us from seeing signs from spirit, so dreams are the easiest route.

Dreams of loved ones can range from brief to long and vivid. If dreams are so vivid that you feel as if you were really there, then it was a visit from spirit and not just a dream.

It is most common that our spirit loved ones appear in a peaceful setting, like a meadow or quiet yard. Others may appear in a home. Spirits convey peaceful places because they want to assure us that they are happy and at peace. They use the visuals of these wonderful, tranquil places to convey those feelings of contentment so we can stop grieving and fretting over them.

If you would like to get a message from your pet or person who passed, before you go to bed, just ask them either aloud or in thought (because sound and thought are energy and they can "hear" and "read" it) to come into your dreams.

In this chapter you'll read of experiences from several people who had dreams or visits from the spirits of their pets.

April's Dreams

April said: *I've had dogs my whole life and have loved all of them. My two most recent dogs were Taz and Porkchop. They were best friends.*

Porkchop died from cancer about four years ago at the age of 13, and Taz died two years ago at the age of 15 1/2 when we put him down because he kept falling and hurting himself and could no longer get around.

I still talk to them while they're in heaven and they often come to me in dreams. I wonder if this is them trying to tell me that they are okay. I miss them so much.

Editor's Note: I explained to April that her dreams are indeed their confirmation that they are okay on the other side.

Scooter Dreams

Brandi said: *I lost my little Scooter 1/29/14. I miss him terribly. When I miss him the most, I have wonderful dreams about him.*

Editor's Note: That's because spirit knows when we are grieving. Since Brandi has accepted Scooter's passing, and the grief isn't acting as a block, it's easier for Scooter to make return appearances in her dreams.

Dreams and a Spirit Influences

Deb said: *I definitely believe (from experience) that they [pets] can touch us even after they die. Quincy, the dog who was the love of my life (had been abused, required extensive rehab) left me devastated after I had him put down due to pancreatic cancer.*

Three nights after Quincy passed he came to me in a dream, a dream so real I woke up thinking he was really there. I felt he had come to me to tell me it was okay and I had made the right decision.

It definitely helped me as I struggled to cope. Before Quincy, I had special things happen after I lost Hammer. He was the most intelligent, insightful dog I have ever known. When things in my life went south, and I needed protection, he chose a side (mine) and never looked back. After I lost Hammer, I would still occasionally hear his bark amongst the voices of my other dogs.

On his [Hammer's] next birthday, I adopted a rescue [Quincy]. It blew my mind when I heard the new boy bark. He had Hammer's voice! And then I noticed his eyes - they were Hammer's eyes. And it wasn't just me, without any prompting, my friend who knew Hammer well said the same thing!

Editor's Note: As I've mentioned before, our dogs that pass lead us to adopt other dogs (when the time is right) and then they will train the new dog to behave the way they did in life. Hammer led Deb to adopt Quincy. Then, Hammer taught Quincy how to bark like he did.

Dreams are the easiest way dogs or human spirits come to us to let us know they're okay on the other side, and still around us as Quincy did for Deb.

Michelle Gets a Visit
Michelle said: *I had dreams that they came to see me where it was so real I could feel the spirit presence. After I had those dreams I felt like it was time for me to grieve and it felt like they wanted closure for me.*

Carol's Dream
I am in the darkness of grief. My dear Bailey was diagnosed with lymphoma at 4 1/2 in March 2013. After 9 months of chemo and 2 remissions she passed away Dec.5, 2013. Into 2014 we got a puppy Bella (7 1/2 months old now) whom we are cherishing fully.
I had a dream that Bailey told me she'd return in a dog with two different colored eyes. Two days later Summer's picture showed up

in my newsfeed saying she was in need of a home (and adopted Summer)! Bailey or not we loved her for her!

(Photo: Bailey (left) and Summer (right) Credit: Carol).

So, we added a new pup named Summer and Bella and Summer became the best of friends and she fit in beautifully.

Five months after losing Bailey we were at routine vet visit, I just gave Summer (3 months old) a treat when a dog appeared around corner startling her, causing her to inhale treat (and choke). Three vets worked on her and could not save her!!

I feel so devastated and guilt ridden. I need a sign! I am just so numb at the moment.

Editor's Note: It's difficult to know why Summer passed so quickly after being adopted, but it was her time. She may have had a congenital health issue.

I reached out to Carol after receiving this email and was able to assure her that she should not feel guilty. Accidents happen and there is nothing we can do to prevent them. Summer was only supposed to be here for a short time. In that time, she was an example that Bailey's spirit was strong and still around.

##

Chapter 8
Spirits Getting Physical

One of the more common ways for spirits to convey their presence is through touch.

As a paranormal investigator, I have felt the touch of Earth-bound ghosts and spirits who have crossed over. Earth-bound ghosts have poked, prodded, gently pushed and brushed by me. Ghosts and spirits have also made me feel the pain of their death (which most people who are not mediums fortunately do not experience) to prove who they are. That said, I've felt heart failure, cancer, stroke, stabbing, gun shot, hit on the head, and even felt as if being pushed down a stair.

Spirits, like those of our pets, provide lighter tactile feelings. In fact, on one paranormal investigation I felt a cat's tail brush up against me and there was no living cat in the house (but the homeowner said she's seen a spirit cat there before).

If your cat or dog used to jump on your bed and sleep with you, you'll likely feel them doing it in spirit, too. Many cat parents I've met have said they have felt the spirit of their cat jump up, lightly walk across the foot of the bed and curl up. Dog parents have reported similar incidents.

Cold spots are another way in which we can "feel" a ghost or spirit. Because they are beings of energy, they take the energy of the motion of molecules of air to "charge themselves" in order to convey their presence. When they remove the energy of motion from fast moving particles of air (warm air), it slows down. Slower moving molecules or air are cold air, thus, we feel a "cold spot" whenever we are in the presence of a ghost or spirit trying to manifest.

This chapter contains three more accounts from people I've met or whom have emailed me about their tactile encounters.

Nuzzled by a Princess

Princess was a beloved family cat who lived with Joanie and her daughter. I met both of them at the Pet Expo and they told me that they created a Facebook page as a tribute to their cat, Princess, who passed. "Paws for Princess" is a grassroots group of caring, compassionate folks in western Massachusetts who are dedicated to the safety and well-being of all community cats.

Princess was a feral kitten who touched many people's lives. She joined our family at 4 months old and lived a happy life. Princess passed suddenly at less than 2 years old. This group was named after her to keep her memory alive and to protect all feral cats.

Joanie's daughter told me that after Princess had passed, she has sensed her beloved cat several times. She said that she had been nuzzled by her cat's spirit, feeling a cat nose on her face and no one was there! She also reported feeling Princess' spirit brush by her legs and she's felt Princess on the bed.

All of these things are ways in which cats commonly communicate from spirit. Cats tend to be more stealth in their after death communications and tend to give physical sensations.

For more information about "Paws for Princess" check out the Facebook page: https://www.facebook.com/PawsForPrincess

Physical Sensations

Jennifer said: Whenever I sleep, I feel something jump up onto my bed when I'm the only one in the room. I also feel gentle nudges on my arm as well.

I lost my dog Chance when I was a little girl. He froze to death outside one winter and there was nobody with him when he died. I'd love to talk to my Chance again and the other pets that I've lost while growing up.

Editor's Note: Chance's death was traumatic to those he left behind, but he came back to Jennifer to let her know that he's okay. I get the sense the Chance laid down in the snow and passed in his sleep. It seems that Chance and some of the other cats and dogs were giving her tactile signs that they're all around her.

Nicole said: *My mom lost her beloved Tessa almost a year ago. She had her mother (Tara) and fell in love with Tessa when the litter was born. Tara raised Tessa through the best 15 years of her life. My mother loves us dearly but Tessa had this chunk of her heart that nothing could or ever will fill again.*

She has spoken of how she feels Tessa curl up at her feet every now and then and it brings tears to her eyes. She knows she is still with her today.

Editor's Note: If you have lost a dog or a cat, be aware that the time in which you will most likely feel their physical presence and touch is when you are in the "twilight" part of your rest. That is, either just before you fall asleep or just as you're waking up.

##

Chapter 9
Noises: Bark, Meow, and more

Our pets can make audible noises to let us know that they are still around us in spirit. Whether it be a bark, growl, meow or purr. Their pets nails can sometimes be heard on a floor, and pet spirits have been heard walking around or going up and down stairs. Some people have reported hearing their pets' collar jingle or have heard their dog "paw" at the door to come inside as they did when they were in the physical world.

The first story in this chapter is a personal experience I had from our dachshund named Sprite. Following Sprite's story are experiences people shared with me on my Facebook pages and my blog. These are grouped together to show the different ways that spirit pets have used noises to communicate with the living.

Our Dog Sprite's Birthday Bark
Sprite's spirit announced he was around in December 2015. Sprite was born on December 23, 1996 (and passed in July 2013), so it was no surprise that he made a vocal appearance in the month of his birth.

One evening after everyone had gone to bed, I heard a soft bark from the kitchen (two rooms away). I immediately called out "Sprite" because it sounded just like his bark! Sprite's bark was unique and at a higher pitch than our other dogs. In fact, it was so high-pitched we used to call it a "squeet." One of the nicknames we had for him was "Squeety."

Immediately, I leaned over the side of my bed and saw our three living dogs all sleeping soundly on their beds, covered in their blankets. Once I realized it was Sprite, I immediately remembered that his birthday was in December. Spirits come around on birthdays, anniversaries and holidays (and other times we need them) to let us know they're still with us - just as Sprite did again.

Pawing at the Door

Erika said: *My fur baby who was only 5 just died from Hemangiosarcoma [cancer of blood vessel walls] 3 weeks ago. He died in our house and I think his spirit is in the house. I hear him paw at my door whenever I'm the only one home and doors swing open.*

Lynn said: *After our dog Kirby passed away, my husband has told me that he's heard her pawing the back door to come in as she used to do.*

Ashley said: *We lost our beagle mix, Bootsie, a few years ago. Her and my dad were extremely close and he says he can still hear her jumping up on the bed and scratching at the door.*

Walking Around

Krisi said: *I swear I hear my beloved American Eskimo Princess who passed away a couple years ago, still walking around the house.*

Nicole said: *I miss my beagle terribly. She passed away last September just two months shy of her 14th birthday. I had her since I was 8 years old. I've had experiences where I've clearly heard her at home and finally dreamt with her / visited her, letting me know she was alright on the other side.*

Nails on the Floor, Collar Jingle

D.B. said: *After my beloved dachshund, Sidney died, I was devastated! I had had him for over 16 years, which is a long life for a dachshund. We had a very special bond between us. He was my* *wonderful, loving animal child. He became ill and I knew his organs were shutting down.*

I was holding onto him and felt him take his last breath, and he had crossed over the Rainbow Bridge. I cried for days, weeks, I missed him so very much! One day, I laid down and was trying to get some rest, when I heard the click of toenails on the floor. I became alert and also heard the jingle of collar tags.

I asked, "Is that you, Sid?" I felt the softest breath on my hand. I knew my Sidney was with me. I told him I knew he was there, and how much I loved him and missed him. I couldn't see him, but I knew without a shadow of a doubt, he was with me. About ten minutes later, I knew he had left. That was four years ago, and I still cry when I think of my boy. I will always miss him.

Jingling Collar
Joanne said: *My 18-month-old male German Shepherd died suddenly 2 years ago and at night you can hear his choker going up and down the stairs.*

Barking, Jingling Collar, Sighting
Bernadette said: *Hi Rob - My dogs who have passed let me know that they are well & still with us. I have heard most of my dogs bark after they have passed. Our family Saint Bernard let us know he was still with us when we would hear his collar tags. My Dad and I actually saw him sitting on the steps on the back porch.*

About 10 years ago I was with a friend who had just lost her work partner, a German Shepherd. We were chatting outside and I heard a dog bark. It was obvious by her expression she had heard it too. I said, "That was...!" She smiled and said that it was [her late dog's bark]. After that, each time one of my dogs would pass over I would hear their bark. It could be a week after they passed or years later.

I also firmly believe that once our dogs pass over they send us our next dogs. I have one now who was sent by my male yellow Lab who loved everyone and my black female Lab that I did Search and Rescue tracking with and competitive obedience. She did not like anyone but my male yellow Lab.

I now have a female yellow Lab who loves everyone is a tracking machine and is preparing for competitive obedience. She came from an elderly person who had my dog and her sister. I went to pick up my Lab. She got up on the chair & laid across my lap. I put on the collar and lead on he she walked out, didn't even look back. Got in the car and has been home with me ever since.

Dog Barks "Warning" in Spirit before Passing

I received the following email from Greta about an unusual happening. Before you read the story, keep in mind that people and apparently pets, can do "astral projections" - meaning their spirits can leave their bodies to give messages.

From: Greta, Apr 4

Hi Mr. Gutro - I lost my best friend, Lucky, on March 6, 2014. He had cancer but lived longer than was expected I think due to me changing his diet and doing all I could for him which led me to your book "Pets and the Afterlife." It really helped me to not feel so sad and guilty. Out of all the books I've read, it helped the most.

During this whole process, a couple of months before his passing, I started hearing a dog bark in my sleep, it sounded as if it was coming from another room and was so real it would wake me out of a sound sleep thinking it was our other dog needing to go out which she rarely does late at night.

The barking was not the voice of our dog who passed either nor were they barking in their sleep because my husband is up late and

46

didn't hear it. The voice was similar to the dog that is still with us and they have 2 distinct voices.

The closer to his passing, the more frequent the barks came then maybe two days before he passed, my husband said he finally heard it too and it sounded like it was right in his face but both dogs were sleeping, they sleep with me and he was sleeping in the living room. I actually thought maybe I was having mental problems. The weird thing is, since his passing I have not heard the barking even once.

I've tried looking it up but only read about people hearing barking dogs after they pass and it is their own dog. This bark was definitely not him who passed. What are your thoughts on this? It really has me baffled!

My Note to Greta:

Dear Greta- Thank you for your note, and my deepest sympathies on the passing of your boy. It sounds like you and your husband actually had a visitation instead of a dream despite the different sound of the bark.

Sometimes, before they pass, the essence of pets, like people, will leave their bodies to communicate with their loved ones and let them know that they will soon pass and cross over. I believe that's what happened with your dog who passed. He was giving you both a message to prepare you that he was going to cross soon. - This is similar to people who experience hearing their grandmother call their name even though they may be across the country, and later learn that their grandmother passed in a day or two.

I've spoken with many people who have had experiences like this. Including this story in my new book is a way to honor Lucky and help others understand that dogs can give us warning signs before they pass, to help us prepare for their passing.

***

To hear a dog's nails on the floor, a bark, meow, or a pawing at the door takes a lot of energy. Spirits are able to make those noises using the emotional energy of love that you share for each other. Don't be disappointed, however, if you do not receive these kinds of signals. Each dog and cat will communicate in their own way, just as they all have their individual personalities.

Some pets may choose to communicate in any of the other ways covered in this book. In addition, I want to reiterate that grief acts as a block to messages from spirits, so be patient.

##

Chapter 10
Send in the Clone (or Look-alike)

One of the interesting ways that spirits convey that they're around us is that they lead us to a "clone" of themselves, or someone that looks like them. In fact, the dog, cat or horse doesn't even need to look exactly like them, perhaps resemble them or make you think of them. These "clones" or doppelgangers are just a way of reminding us that the spirits of our pets are still around us.

Doppelganger's Perfect Timing

In September 2014, I traveled to the Boston area where I had a booth at the New England Pet Expo in Wilmington, Massachusetts. Once I was set up at my table, it didn't take long for the first dog's spirit to send a message to his mom.

A woman named Donna came to my booth and talked with me and Ruthie Larkin (the Beantown Medium) about the passing of her Black French Bulldog, Basil. She said that she was looking for a sign from Basil and missed him more than anything. Donna felt comfort from learning some of the ways that dogs will communicate from the other side.

No sooner than I told her that dogs will sometimes lead to their pet parents other dogs that look just like them than a Black French Bulldog came marching down the aisle toward Donna!

Clearly Basil orchestrated his doppelganger's appearance while Donna was at my booth. And the dog showed up right after I told her about pets use doppelgangers to tell their parents they are still with them in spirit. It was amazing!

*(Photo: A black French bulldog at the New England Pet Expo.
Credit: R. Gutro)*

I received the following story by email:

Cat Doppelganger
Diane said: *We had a family cat that passed away of old age. I was not able to see him before passing. He was the sweetest kitty that was greatly missed.*

About one month after he passed, I just happened to be thinking about him. It was 10:30 at night and I was driving through a small town. I pulled the car over to the side of the street, waiting for a friend. While sitting in the car, not a person nor car came past. Across the street and a bit down the road I saw a small animal walking towards my direction. As it was getting closer to me I could see it was a cat. My sensing of our kitty had become very strong at This point. This cat looked exactly like our beloved family kitty. It came all the way up to my car door. When I opened my door to get out, it seemed to get very happy. As I gazed down at him, he just stared at me purring. While petting him I realized that "somehow" this could be our beloved cat.

He was allowing me to say goodbye (something which I couldn't do before [and wanted to]). I called him by name, told him we missed him. We stood by each other for a while. It was like he was telling me he's alright. I thanked him for allowing me to say goodbye he slowly turned and walked away. It was amazing.

Cats and dogs will bring other cats or dogs to us that strongly resemble them to give us the peace to say goodbye, or let us know they're still around us.

##

Chapter 11
Return Appearances

In Chapter 4, I discussed how the spirits of our dogs and cats are capable of physical manifestation for short periods of time. Children are the most susceptible to seeing spirits because their logical minds have not fully developed so they don't dismiss what they see so readily. However, some adults who are more sensitive to spirits will also be able to see them.

Earlier in the book I touched on the fact that dogs and cats can see ghosts and spirits because of the different configuration of cones and rods in their eyes that allow them to see faster movement. Spirits and ghosts move at that higher vibration. Sometimes our pets' spirits may not be able to visibly appear, but we can sense them. The following are experiences that people have shared with me on my Facebook pages and my blog. These are grouped together to show the different ways that spirit pets have made appearances to communicate with the living.

Dog Spirit Sightings
Kristin Said: *Kenyon passed in 2008 and I still ear a locket with some of his fur in it. I believe that I have seen him a few times over the years and it has made me happy to think he is still beside us.*

Dogs- Visible To Kids
Anna said: *I lost my 4 year-old Husky last year. And earlier this week, my 3 year-old son said he saw her playing with our Boxer. I miss her deeply.*

Editor's Note: Children have the ability to see ghosts and spirits because they have not developed their logical minds, and don't explain things away. They just accept what they see.

Cat Appearances

Carolyn said: *I lost my beautiful Tabby, Missy, a year ago yesterday. I've always felt her around me and have glimpsed her out of the corner of my eye so many times since she passed. Sometimes I smell her, hear her and feel her. I'd love to be able to prove to myself and my family that I'm not going crazy and there are actually other people who have had the same experiences as me. If people believe in talking to human members of their family, surely our furry babies will try and make contact to.*

Dogs Sensed In a Room: Our Dog Sprite

In a previous chapter I mentioned that our Dachshund, Sprite who passed in 2013 provided us with a bark in 2015 during the month of his birth. Sprite also provided us with a butterfly on several occasions and appeared as a shadow in his favorite place.

Several times, both my partner and I have seen a small shadow near the front door of the house. It is Sprite. Sprite used to sit and look out the glass storm door at the squirrels that played in the front yard, or the cars that drove down the street. We know that he still likes to do that. Dogs in spirit continue to enjoy doing the same things they did in the physical.

Following are stories from others who have also sensed the spirit of their dogs.

Tracey said: *Recently lost my dog Hunter and I'm having a really hard time with it. I want to believe he is happy and free of pain. There are times I have sensed him in a room with us would love to know more.*

Dar said: *I lost my beloved fur friend Seth of 12 years (3.5 years ago he passed). One day as I was laying on the couch with a migraine he came to me in spirit and said to me "get another dog."*

That was 2.5 years ago and now I have another best friend. This is all because of my boy Seth. I can feel his gentle presence every once in a while. I miss his gentle loving nature so much.

Sensing, Seeing and Hearing a Dog's Spirit

Aleta said: *Hello Rob, I'm currently listening to Paranormal Review Radio's most recent interview with you about pets in the afterlife. I lost my dog Max in November of 2011, a week after we got our puppy Maya. He had gotten sick the day before we were to pick her up from the animal shelter and over a course of a week his health declined.*

I felt the moment his health turned that his time on this Earth was coming to an end and I couldn't stop crying or took anyone's assurances that he will recover to heart. I just knew. To make matters even more complicated during this period, I had a new little one to raise and I felt so guilty taking care of her. In my mind, I thought Max felt he was being replaced. The puppy needed care and attention . . . so did he.

On Friday we came home from work and found Maximus next to the puppy's crate. He looked awful. But stood to greet us, happy as if to say, "I'm glad you all are home. Me and the kid talked, I think she'll be fitting in quite nicely." It was almost like he was passing on the torch and he knew the race was coming to an end. Well, tell that to the humans. We sped to the vet for his scheduled appointment that evening (the puppy's too) and were told that he was dying. I signed the papers to put him down. I couldn't watch, so my mother stayed with him. I couldn't sleep in my bedroom or go upstairs, every turn and corner reminded me of him. His things were bagged up that very night because I couldn't take it.

For eleven years he had been my best friend and now he was gone like everyone else. I had lost two very important members of my family not that long ago and Max was the straw that killed the camel's back.

The next morning I had awakened in a daze. But I hoping it wasn't real and that he'd pop up in greeting like he usually did in the mornings, sniffing loudly. Sometimes he liked to grumble too, when I didn't get up fast enough. :-) He had a big personality and was extremely funny. I personally thought that he believed he was human.

I laid in bed for a moment with my back turned to the window and suddenly I felt a soft little presence behind me. My eyes closed, I knew everyone was still asleep. I laid a little longer and the presence began to move as if sniffing. Just like Max! I felt so happy and told him thank you. Then the encounter was over. He came to tell him that he was OK and I was (still am) grateful for it. Of course, I will always miss him but I'm glad to know that he is fine.

Earlier this year I had done a Water ITC experiment for the very first time. I had asked Max to come through if he could and he did! I was rather surprised because I had thought Water ITC's were questionable. Not only did he make an appearance but other animals as well. Why do you think that was? I saw a wolf-like creature, a kitten, and a cat. It was something. I've done another ITC experiment in April and that one was a little troubling, I had to seek help with cleansing. I'd much rather deal with the animals if you know what I mean and I'm not going to do anymore experiments. But from the Max session, I'd like to show you what I had captured. It was very interesting.

Also, the evening of the day of that session, I had seen Max walking down the hall along with other spirits. It appears it is true when you are aware of them and are able to communicate with them others come. Mind you, that sort of freaked me out. Rather deal with the one's you know, lol. Not everyone was good in life, if you get my drift.

56

(Photo: Max on May 1, 2012. Credit: Aleta)

But since the cleansing, all (weird) activity has stopped and I haven't seen anything. I haven't dealt with the paranormal since I was a child and early teens, so I was freaked out.

But I'm glad to have gotten a chance to listen to your interview and of course, I teared about when you were talking about Sprite and I'm so happy that your loved ones were there to help him cross over.

By the way, why is it when I was sensing and seeing spirits why hasn't my little dog been responding? Or has she and I wasn't paying much attention? I think she has but I put it off as her selling woof tickets. Lol!
Thanks, Aleta

Editor's Note: Aleta most definitely received amazing signs from Max. As for her other dog not responding, sometimes pets become so used to spirits, either human or animal, that they look at them as others living in the house, so they disregard them!

##

Chapter 12
Q&A About a Pet's Ashes

In my first "Pets" book, I mentioned that if you have a pet's or a person's ashes, there may be some residual energy attached to them which can serve as a draw or a magnet to attract their energy. However, since most people and pets are cremated or buried in whole form, their spirit still finds us because they are tuned into our energy.

I received a question from someone who felt guilty about not keeping their pet's ashes. If you don't keep your pet's ashes, you need not feel as if you should. It's an individual choice. Whether you bury your pets remains or keep the ashes, it matters not, as their spirit will always find you. It's the love that you share that acts as a beacon to spirit and draws them to you.

It works the same way with human spirits. Most people's bodies are buried or cremated. Cremated remains are placed in urns, buried or scattered. It doesn't matter where the remains are located, because the love that you share with the person connects you from this life to the afterlife.

Question: *The ashes of my dog were put into a communal cremation, and I am struggling with guilt. What can you tell me?*

My response: There is no need to feel any guilt or anxiety about placement of her ashes in a communal cremation. They were just remnants of a physical existence.

The souls of our pets and people leave their physical body usually even just before their physical body dies. The ashes are just the remnants of a physical shell, and it's not necessary to keep them. They have a small amount of residual energy, but that fades over time, and a connection to them fades over time. What doesn't fade is the bond of energy (of love) you share, that will always keep you connected.

My partner and I have the ashes of our dogs and we will have them placed with ours when our time comes. Again, it's an individual choice.

In 1967, my parents opted to have their Cocker Spaniel cremated, and didn't accept the ashes. Of course, things were different in the 1960s. In 1993, when their poodle, Gigi passed, they had her cremated and bought her a plot in a pet cemetery which happens to be about 20 miles away from where they are now buried.

Regardless, the spirit of your pet will be linked to you because of the bond (energy) of love you share. That also means that wherever you go in the physical plane (here on Earth), they'll find you. If you move from one house to another, or go on travel, your love for them acts as a beacon that enables them to find you.

###

Chapter 13
Scents from Spirits

Spirits can use sounds, touch, appear visibly, move things, manipulate electrical things and even make an appearance as a scent.

I've spoken with many people who have smelled their late mom's favorite perfume whenever they were thinking of their mother, or a cigar on the birthday of their favorite uncle who used to smoke them. Spirits of people are not the only ones who can give us "scented" signs. Pets can, too.

When I was at a pet expo, I met a woman named Gail who told me her dog had gone outside and passed near a rosebush the day of his passing. She told me when she went out soon after calling her dog, she quickly found that he had passed away near roses. She said she will never forget the smell of the roses.

After she had her dog cremated, she got the ashes and smelled roses. She knew that her dog was giving her a sign that he was still around. Gail told me whenever she smells roses, she gets a strong feeling that her dog's spirit is right beside her.

##

Part 2:
Messages I Received from Pets

In this part of the book, I will share messages that I received from people's dogs or cats. Dogs and cats can convey messages, images, and words that they heard during their time on Earth in the physical.

Like human spirits, they use things that are unique to them to identify who they are and / or whom they are connected with.

In chapter 14, you'll read about a dog named Buddy that not only showed me where his favorite place was, but told me the name of someone else that he enjoyed spending time with. Along with those, additional signs from Buddy helped prove that he is still with his pet parents from time to time.

Although this section is filled with stories about how I as a medium received messages from people's dogs or cats, anyone can recognize the signs that I outlined in the previous section.

Chapter 14
The Most Detailed Message from an Incredible Dog

In October, 2014, I was invited to give a talk at the Tysons-Pimmit Library in Falls Church, Virginia. The talk was well-attended and I sensed that there were some pet spirits in the room. Afterwards, a married couple came up to me and told me about their intense grief over the loss of their dog, Buddy. Buddy had passed two months before and they were struggling with their grief.

I didn't hear from Buddy when I was talking with them, but I certainly heard from him later. In fact, Buddy gave me more details, images and even a name to prove that his spirit was still around his mom and dad from time to time.

That evening when I returned home, I received and email from Buddy's parents Brett and Daniela. Because of the amazing signs and confirmations, they have graciously allowed me to share the story in this book.

In this chapter you'll read the email exchanges between myself and Brett and Daniela, and the amazing confirmations. They even provided photographic proof that the images Buddy showed me from his memories.

The First Email
From: Brett   Date: Oct 11, 2014
Hi Rob, Thank you for your wonderful discussion today at the Tysons-Pimmit Regional Library. We will be reading your book "Pets and the Afterlife" from cover to cover.

I thank you for your kindness and understanding in speaking with us and giving us a hug – we have been emotional wrecks for the last 55 days since making the decision to let our 15½ year-old puppy go.

(Photo: Buddy. Credit: Brett and Daniela)

Following up on what I asked, I respectfully ask for any sign or sense that you would have about whether our dog Buddy is Ok. It is difficult for me to ask this favor, but depth of our loss and experiencing your honesty and sincerity drive me to ask for your assistance.

We were both deeply impressed with your lecture. Your discussion of radio and music confirmed what I already knew. When my father passed away in 2009, I was in Germany. As I was travelling to the funeral, I found myself driving along the highway (autobahn) in Bavaria, listening to German folk music on the radio and getting tired. Suddenly, an amazingly obscure song that only had meaning to my Dad and I played on a German radio station that would never play that song under ordinary circumstances. It was so clearly a sign from him that he was OK.

My wife and I both left your discussion today knowing that you are a wonderful human being. And thank you for all of your efforts to take care of dogs – which my wife and I refer to as "Angels on Earth."
Kind Regards, Brett and Daniela

From: Rob Gutro - October 12, 2014

Hi Brett and Daniela - Thanks for the email. - It was really great to meet you, and it was Buddy's spirit that led you to discover the talk yesterday at the library. He wanted you to be there to help you get over the intense grief by learning how to recognize signs that he's still around you.

Last night before I went to bed, Buddy did come through to me. Of course, as I mentioned during the talk, it was when I was taking a shower- and my mind was clear.

He told me that you agonized over making a decision and cried a lot. He said you did the right thing. He doesn't hurt anymore. He also said that you have his ashes. Do you?

When he came to me he was peaceful and happy, and healthy again. He kept telling me to "ask dad about ice cream" and that he treasured his time here, but it was his time to go. He said that he taught you both unconditional love and that gift needs to be shared with another pup when the time is right for you. Of course, he will guide you to find the right one when you're ready. He said you still have a toy or toys of his, and he would like you to keep them for when you adopt again.

The intense grief you feel should be turned around into remembering the pure love he brought to you both. Take the pictures out that you have together and put them in an electronic frame to keep showing you the happy times together. He wants you to celebrate the time, not grieve over it. He says "you had a great time together, and I want to be remembered that way."

There are specific things that he showed me. One was that he was walking on what looked like a long gravel path or trail in a wooded area. I saw big trees, very tall, and there was also a home near the woods. He showed me that he's happily walking through the forested trails.

I also sensed a woman there with him, and heard "Elsa, Elisa," Eliza, or Lisa" -it sounded like it was far away, so I can't sure of the exact name. Does it make any sense to you? - She also had light-colored hair, either blonde or white/grey... I also saw a man on the other side with a beard. Both were with him, walking peacefully and all were happy.

Buddy is with your relatives on the other side, and being well cared for there as he was here.

He wants to thank you for giving him the greatest life he could imagine. He showed me that he was partially covered by a blanket with his face sticking out, panting with a smile, and tongue hanging out. He said he was really spoiled- in a great way!

He DOES still visit you from time to time. He showed me a rectangular bed or mattress at the end of your bed. He said that he comes when you're sleeping and sits at the end of your bed to protect you both.

Wow. That's a lot of messages from your boy. Just know that his love still connects him to you, and he wants you to change the grief to a more positive thing- remembering him and the time you had together. He said you have to share all that love for him with another dog that will greatly benefit by it, but that he's always going to be in your heart. He said he'll even help train the new family member. :)

Please let me know if any of these things make sense to you- and I hope you find comfort in all the messages he provided. I wrote them down last night on a piece of paper after getting out of the shower and it was late, but I think I got them all!
Rob Gutro

(Photo: Buddy and Daniela. Credit: Brett S.)

Confirmations of Buddy's Signs
From: Brett and Daniela
Date: Sun, 12 Oct 2014
Hi Rob,

Thank you so much. Everything you have said makes sense: I did cry a lot in the week before the day he left us and agonized greatly over the decision. He declined over many years and declined

69

rapidly at the end.   But I never cried like the week before and since. You have seen differently, but I am usually one to not show emotions.

On the night before his passing, we took him to a dog park so he could watch other dogs play from the comfort of his mat and blanket in the car. Afterwards, we all bought Wendy's Ice Cream. Wow did he love that. Ice cream was his last big treat. He was definitely an ice cream junky during his life.

After the lecture, my wife pointed out that two roses were blooming from an old rosebush right next to where I placed his ashes. The rosebush is very old but amazingly two fresh branches have appeared with a rose on each - just after I put his ashes in the ground with a football, laser pointer, and other little puppy artifacts.

We have kept his little orange and brown chicken toy that he loved so much. And we'll give it to our next dog.

My parents-in-law live in that house near the woods in Germany. The never-ending woods with gigantic trees are about twenty yards away. Elke (sounds like Elsa when my German father-in-law yells it) is my mother-in-law. She has blond hair that is mixed with light grey. And my wife explains that her middle name is Elizabeth which I did not know.

We used to always visit them, then go on a big walk through the woods along the trail with the very high trees. Those trees are in the Thüringen Wald. When my wife and I lived in Germany and visited the U.S.A., Buddy would stay with my parents-in-law and be immensely spoiled. After three weeks we returned once to see that he had gotten plump with the countless stream of sausage that Elke gave him. They are still alive and take big long walks along the wooded path you are talking about. It starts as a gravel path and eventually turns into a pure wooded trail. So, Buddy is accompanying them on their daily walks today. His favorite times were always right there walking through the woods and playing with the whole family.

(Photo: The actual forested path Buddy loved walking through. Credit: Brett and Daniela S.)

I am guessing that the man with a beard would be my father in his young man form. As we paid for a dog sitter when my wife and I were working, we can also guess that the man with the Beard is a friend that Buddy made while we were busy working. Buddy had lots of friends we never met. It is a hilarious memory for my wife and I when we drove into the German village we lived in and discovered that Buddy was being walked by a family we had never met.

In Buddy's heyday, we lived in Germany and I spent countless hours walking with him in the woods. That was our magical time together. I have been dreaming of our time there. We are so happy that he has found his way back home. Thank you so much. Brett and Daniela

From: Rob Gutro - October 12, 2014

Brett and Daniela- Thank you for writing back. I'm always amazed at the clarity of messages from spirit, and Buddy provided much more detail than any other dog's spirit I've ever communicated with. What an amazing and smart boy! Thanks for the picture of Buddy - what a handsome boy.

How cool to see the map of his favorite trails and the area he was telling me about!

But Buddy is something special. The people, the ice cream (btw, we have never given our dogs ice cream because we're both lactose intolerant, so we can't enjoy it- so I thought it odd Buddy mentioned ice cream)., the descriptions of the places - all amazing.

I'm so excited that he's been able to come through and provide these signs to you that he's well, happy, energetic and watching over you.

Thanks, Rob Gutro

Another Confirmation about the Forest Path

Brett and Daniela sent me more information about the forested path that Buddy told me about, and provided photos:

Whenever we went on long walks through the woods, our family would slowly drift apart with the long-legged men of the family moving ahead and Elke and Daniela pulling up the rear. Buddy had the herding instinct and always performed the "rear guard" role – staying close to the last member of our family – Elke. So the distant and muted "Elke" calls were from her husband Klaus Peter W. My wife read your email and also confirmed this independently. Attached is a photo of Daniela's family doing their almost daily walk through the beautiful woods of Thüringen.

(Photo: Daniela's family walking through Thüringen Forest Credit: Brett and Daniela).

Here is a photo of "a long gravel path or trail in a wooded area [with] big trees, very tall" – Just FYI, you won't find these tall trees in Germany if you drive just 40 to the north or 40 miles to the south. They are unique to Thüringen Forest and the Black Forest.

(Photo: Elke Elizabeth W. - Buddy's Grandma who took him on many walks through the large forested areas. Credit: Brett and Daniela S.)

A Note of Thanks

From Brett & Daniela Shelley

Hi Rob, I am also amazed. I am so grateful to you for giving us the good word that Buddy is ok. Thank you so much! Also, giving us a hug was about the nicest thing anyone has done for us in a long time. Brett

(Photo: Aerial view of the forest Buddy loved walking through. Credit: Brett and Daniela)

Rob, you are most certainly welcome to share this amazing story with your readers and audiences. No need to change our names. You have our permission and full rights to eternalize Buddy's life and memory.

I have attached two photos and will send some more. The two attached to this are photos of Elke Elizabeth Wehr – Buddy's Grandma. She watched over Buddy many times and was his 3rd favorite person in the world. You'll already seen her. The really tall trees you've seen around this area are shown in the 3rd photo.
Brett and Daniela

****

Buddy not only provided me with the name of his grandma, and a physical description of her, but a visible image of his favorite walking path and giant trees. He shared what happened on his last day in the physical plane - his blanket and the ice cream, his favorite treat.

This is great proof of how a dog knows words/language, names, and remembers places and the loving things we do with them. They are bound to us forever.

##

Chapter 15
Many Signs and Confirmations from Poopy

At the end of May, 2015, I received a message through my Facebook page from John and Diana M. asking for some sign from their Chihuahua who passed days before.

Often when I read emails and am at peace, I get messages from spirits, and they will give me words, pictures or visuals. As I previously mentioned, human spirits will sometimes come in with pets to help complete a message. That happened as I was reading John's message to me, and that human spirit's appearance with their dog (in spirit) was confirmed by a dream John's brother had.

Here are the series of un-edited emails that went back and forth between us, so that you can see the details provided to me from the human spirit (John's mother) and their Chihuahua.

What's amazing is that every message I received was understood and confirmed. Months after the first email, I received another note that confirmed Poopy was still alive and well in spirit in John's house.

From John:
Hi, Our little Chihuahua, Poopy, passed away on the 24th of May, a few days ago, We are heartbroken and wonder how we can get a message from him. Or if he's okay on the other side. John and Diana Munoz, email me please at   Thank you.

From Rob Gutro - May 30
Hi John and Diana- So sorry for your loss.
On July 7, our dog Sprite (Dachshund) had a tumor burst in his nose that led to bleeding, and the next day we had to make the decision

for him, so I understand what you've experienced with Poopy. You did the right thing, and the most unselfish act of love. He is on the other side, and knows what you did for him. The love he has radiates for you both.

There's an older woman on the other side, short, wearing glasses, grey/white hair, a blue dress and an open sweater over the top of the dress. She has black shoes - "grandmother" or "great grandmother" of one of yours. She's with Poopy. She's provided a very clear vision of herself. Poopy is on her right side, sitting. Looking straight ahead. The woman said "not to worry, Poopy is safe." It almost sounds like she has an accent. Does any of this make sense?

Poopy told me that there's a toy of his that squeaks that he liked near the end of his time. He wants you to keep it and not share it, but put it with his picture. He may squeak it for you sometime to let you know he's there. You'll hear him walking around at night, too, he tells me it will be more like "prancing around." I hear little feet/nails in my head, like he is jumping up on the other side, and turning around.

Poopy will come to visit you from time to time, but will safely be with that older woman who he is standing with.

Who is the other dog that he's familiar with? That dog will be able to see him whenever he visits - even if you're at someone else's home.

I hope you can make sense of these. Just know that he is safe, and will come back from time to time, and appreciates the amazing care and love you shared.
Rob Gutro

From John - May 31

Dear Rob. The other dog is " Charlie " Poopy's little friend, and you're right, Poopy has a long bone-like fur squeaky toy that he hated for Charlie to play with. The older woman is my Mom who passed away from cancer in Dec. last year.

(Photo: Poopy. Credit: John M.)

Twice I was thinking about Poopy and crying, when I went to go out my room, there was a small bird feather on the tile floor, this has happened twice. Thank you for your amazing gift to me and Diana, as it put a big smile on our face. God Bless you and if you can give me news about him from time to time, it would be great. John.

From John - May 31

(This is an amazing email where his brother's dream confirms the messages and images I was given. - Rob)

Rob, this is a message my sister sent me today, "Oil" is my Brother. John

John - Oil told me yesterday that he had a dream of mom holding your little dog. She was saying don't worry I'll take care of him, she was holding him and petting him. She was standing with pop and tippy. How weird.

From John

Also, another confirmation, one that made me cry - is when you wrote he is walking about, and that he said it was more like "prancing." There was this way he would walk up to us when he was happy, shuffling his feet from side to side and his head. And I would always ask him, " are you prancing little boy ". So thank you for that image.

From Rob

That's awesome! - BTW, I realized the reason I was told "grandmother" was that's how he knew your mom!

Thank you for the confirmations. I'm so sorry about your mom's passing, too. It's not strange at all that your brother had a dream of your mom holding Poopy! That's just a confirmation of the same images she gave me! - And what a great confirmation Poopy gave through that dog toy. Dogs communicate through things that they are familiar with. Your note back brought a tear to my eyes. I'm so happy that I was able to connect for you! Rob

From John

Yes Rob, please include Our Poopy in your new book, we would love to honor him that way, just let me know what you need. And thank you again, last night I was finally able to sleep well. You're a god send indeed. John and Diana.

Dogs in Spirit Training Other Dogs

Months later, Poopy was still at work in John and Diana's house. I learned that when I received the following email from John on September 6, 2015:

From John

Hi Rob, I hope you've been fine. It's me, John, Poopy's Dad. I just wanna know a couple of things. Is there really a place like Rainbow

Bridge? And lately my other small doggie, (Charlie), has been paying a lot more attention to my wife, Diana. He even crawls under the covers like Poopy used to do, and he never use to do that. Also, he won't let me out of his site, whenever I get up he does too.

Thanks for all Rob and I'm looking forward to your new book. Signed, Poopy's Dad, John

From Rob

Hi John! Good to hear from you! The rainbow bridge is actually an idea that people created, but it's a great vision that helps us understand the peace experienced by spirit. So, we can think of rainbows and get a sense of the beauty and wonder. It's a nice vision for those of us who are trying to understand what spirit experiences.

Thanks for sharing that note about Charlie's change in behavior. That's actually very clear sign that Poopy is teaching him to do EXACTLY what Poopy did when he was here in the physical! So, take comfort in knowing that although you may not see Poopy, he's giving Charlie direction! That's pretty wonderful.

****

In summary, John and Diana were able to confirm every message I received from both their dog Poopy and John's mother (Poopy's "grandma"). From the prancing to the special squeaky toy bone he wanted to keep from the other dog, "Charlie," to the dream his brother had showing the same images that both Poopy and John's mother conveyed to me.

##

Chapter 16
Clancy's Revelation and Message to All Pet Parents

In June 2015, I received an email from Elizabeth (not her real name) who was distraught after the passing of her beloved dog, Clancy. She wanted to know what caused the passing of her young dog and wrote me to help with an answer.

After reading Elizabeth's email, I was able to get a message from Clancy that identified the cause of his passing - which made sense to Elizabeth.

Clancy's answer should also serve as a caution to all pet parents to check their surroundings and make them "pet safe."

In this chapter, you'll read Elizabeth's initial email and my response with the messages I received from Clancy's spirit.

Elizabeth's Email Request
On Sunday, May 31, 2015 at 11:16 PM Elizabeth wrote:
Dear Mr. Gutro, I recently purchased your book, Pets and the Afterlife through Amazon because we lost our baby Clancy on May 19th and I am trying to make sense of the loss and find comfort.

After I started to read your book, I was tempted on so many occasions to email you. However, I am sure that you get many emails a day from grieving pet owners and I am just one of many. I am taking a chance because I want to find out if it is at all possible to have some closure to our tragic story.

Clancy turned one on January 2nd. He was as spunky as his red fur and as sweet and loving as any dog I have ever had. He was my shadow, always by my side. He brought so much light and purpose to mine and my husband's lives.

On May 19th, Clancy had had a fun filled day. He went visiting over at our friends' house and played with his sister dog and our friend's dog. We came home and he played in our pool and then played some more in the pool after my husband came home from work. I knew he was tired so I put him in his crate for a nap and went to my neighbor's house for a dinner party. Everything was fine when I left.

(Photo: Clancy. Credit: Elizabeth)

Around 8:30 p.m. I received a frantic call from my husband that Clancy was crying, screaming in pain and he needed me to come home. I was home within a couple of minutes and Clancy was clearly in pain. He tried to curl up to me to get comfortable, even crawling up my shoulder and sitting on my neck and shoulder.

We contacted two different Veterinarians we use for our dogs. Both said that he probably pulled something while playing in the pool and to give him baby aspirin and place him in his crate so that he can't *move around too much. I placed towels and blankets around him in his crate and gave him the baby aspirin. He calmed down and seemed comfortable. I brought sheets and blankets out and made myself a bed to lie next to him throughout the night to keep an eye on him. I then went to take a quick bath. When I got out of the bath and dressed for bed.*

I went back to his crate to look in on him. This was around 10 or 10:30 p.m. I looked in and he was looking up at me. I looked again and he wasn't breathing. I yelled for my husband and he started CPR to no avail. It was a complete nightmare.

My husband and I are beside ourselves with guilt. We keep thinking that we should have insisted on bringing him to the vet, I feel so guilty that he died in his crate without his mama. I just wish that I could have been holding him when he took his last breath so he knew that I loved him.

We opted not do a necropsy as we were too upset and I could not stand the thought of his little body going through that. However, I wish we would have so that we could have some closure as to what happened to him.

I read in your book about talking to your deceased dog, which I do every day. His ashes are in our house and I kiss his little urn throughout the day.

I don't get the sense that his spirit is here but I do want to make sure that he has crossed over and that he isn't stuck here because of how he died. I also hope that he knows how much we love him and that he doesn't feel like we let him down.

Thank-you for reading this and thank-you for any insight that you can give me.
Elizabeth

Clancy Comes Through to Me
On Mon, Jun 1, 2015 I was sitting at my desk at home and read Elizabeth's email. As I started responding Clancy's spirit came through and brought a powerful message.

Hi Elizabeth - Thank you for your note. I'm so sorry about Clancy's passing. As I started to read your email this morning around 5:30 a.m., I did get a message from Clancy. He indicated that he passed from ingesting a poisonous plant and that it was entirely his fault.

I'm unsure which plant it was, and it may not be in your yard. Here's a list from the ASPCA: https://www.aspca.org/pet-care/animal-poison-control/toxic-and-non-toxic-plants

Clancy wants you to know that it was by ingesting the plant that he passed. Taking him to the vet would not have helped. Because of the plant that he ate there was nothing you could do.

FYI- If you do see a dog eating a toxic plant, give them a teaspoon of hydrogen peroxide to throw up, followed by rushing him to the vet to see if they could do anything (they couldn't in this case).

He was crying because the poison was hurting him inside. He wants you to know that it's NOT your fault. It was his time to move on. He was only supposed to be with you a short time- and his passing was meant to bring you and your husband closer together.

He has crossed over. As he passed, he showed me an older bald man waiting for him outside his crate, to take his spirit into the light (Heaven, Valhalla, Paradise or whatever you wish to call it). The man looked into Clancy's crate (that you lined with blankets) and told him it would be okay, and to come out and walk with him. The older man was bald on top of his head with hair on the sides of his head. I saw him squinting into Clancy's crate and speaking softly to move on with him. The man is related to you or your husband. So, Clancy is on the other side.

Clancy also knows that you kiss his ashes, and doesn't want you to feel guilty. Again, he stresses it was his own fault. If you still have the blanket that he was wrapped in, in the crate please put it around his ashes. He will visit you both from time to time.

I hope you can understand that he wants you not to feel guilt, and is thankful for the love you share (and always will bind you together). He will be waiting for you when it's your time, too.

Dogs and cats on the other side encourage us to adopt again (when ready) and give another homeless pet the love that they experienced. Clancy said that he'll lead you to the right dog when the time is right.

I hope that you find some peace and comfort. He's a beautiful boy, and he's bound to you both forever.
Sincerely,
Rob Gutro

Elizabeth Confirms Clancy's Messages
On Mon, Jun 1, Elizabeth wrote me back, and understood the message from Clancy.

Dear Mr. Gutro, Thank-you, thank-you, thank-you! You have given me such peace.

After looking at the ASPCA site I now know that we have all kinds of poisonous plants around our house that I had NO idea are lethal to dogs. He loved to eat just about any plant or leaf he could get to.

I just wish I had known ahead of time. Now I know and will be able to protect our other dog and future dogs. You have no idea how much this helps me.

Clancy's Important Message to all Pet Parents

Clancy's message was an important one to all pet parents. There are a lot of plants around our homes that may be toxic to our cats and dogs. I was surprised to see that Aloe, Amaryllis, Paperwhites are poisonous plants on the list. I was also surprised to see macadamia nuts on the list. However, I wasn't surprised to see chocolate (the darker the chocolate the more toxic), raisins, grapes, and prunes. There are over 1,000 plants on the list and some of them are likely around your house.

The American Society for the Prevention of Cruelty to Animals or ASPCA has a website about 1,005 toxic plants can be found at: https://www.aspca.org/pet-care/animal-poison-control/toxic-and-non-toxic-plants

If you think that your animal is ill or may have ingested a poisonous substance, the ASPCA urges you to contact your local veterinarian or the ASPCA's 24-hour emergency poison hotline directly at 1-888-426-4435.

Clancy's message is a clear one for all pet parents: please take the time to investigate the plants around your house and protect your pets.

##

Chapter 17
Toesh Conveys How He Passed

Some of the emails I receive from grieving pet parents question how their pet passed. In some cases a pet will pass at home and the parent will never know how or why. Pet parents who lose their pets in this manner have told me that their vets have offered to do an autopsy, but the parents have always refused. After all, these dogs and cats are our children.

In this case, Tracey emailed me in August, 2015 and told me that her cat "Toesh" passed away and didn't know why. She hoped that I would get an answer from "Toesh" and I did. It was an answer that made sense.

Email from Tracey - Jul 24
Rob, my dear Kitty passed away last week, which came as a total surprise to us because we had no idea he was even sick. I know you have a great skill of connecting to animals, so I thought I'd pass this on to you to see if you "get anything" on or from him. If you don't have time, I do understand. Thanks so much! I love reading your [blogs]!

From: Rob Gutro - Aug 12
Tracey - I'm getting a sense that he had renal failure. - Kidneys. Was he urinating a lot? Of course, it may be hard to notice with a litter box... but did you notice him drinking more often?

From: Tracey - Aug 12
I didn't notice, but yes, he did have renal failure. We learned this was this smell he had on his breath, but didn't smell it until the evening he was passing.

(Photo: Toesh. Credit: Tracey Jones Dickerson)

From: Rob Gutro - Aug 13

Thanks for confirming the message. It's amazing how pets can tell me what they passed from- and they know that because they heard it being said when they were alive (in case you were wondering how a cat knows what kidney failure means). -

From: Tracey - Aug 13

Thank you! Sure, you can include it... As for his name, (to spare you the story of thinking he was a she originally naming "her" Precious), we mainly just called him "Kitty," but my sons also called him "Toesh."

##

Chapter 18
Tink's Messages: Feet, Bird, and Male Contemporary

In this chapter you'll read how a dog named Tink came through to me and was able to provide unique messages that proved his identity and that he was still around his mom. Dogs and cats convey images to mediums that they see when they are in physical form. Tink conveyed his obsession with watching his mom's feet, told me of a bird that would signal his presence and how he is with a man who is a contemporary, or same age range as his mom.

As you read the email conversations below, you'll see how Tink's mom proves the messages that he provided me.

Email from Michelle - June 5, 2015
Subject: Still no sign he's still around
Hi Rob, I live in the U.K. and I just watched you on the show "Do you believe "on YouTube and I loved your interview. You were so informative regarding pets that have passed over.

I lost my beautiful dog February 20th, it was very sudden and unexpected and I blame myself. I shouldn't have taken him to the vets that day because he died on the vets table. There was no warning. He was only getting his ears checked to make sure his ear infection had cleared. He died in an instant.

I have been grieving ever since. He was my best friend and companion. He brought me so much joy and love.

I find it difficult to think of him as the pain is too much to bear. He was a Jeanette Chihuahua and he was only 8 years old, his name was Tink.

I talk to him all the time and we had such a strong connection that I was sure he would have let me know he was still around by now.

I miss him so much. I still cry most days. I'm heartbroken. I just want him to know I love him and I'm so sorry I took him to the vets that day. I'm sure if I hadn't taken him he would still be here now. He hated going to the vets, it made him so nervous and he was always afraid.

I miss him so, so much. Rob, do you think he might visit me *at all? Will I ever see him again? I do hope so.*
He was my everything.
Kindest Regards, Michelle

From Rob Gutro - Jun 7

Hi Michelle- I'm so sorry about the passing of Tink. It seems that there was something that was not right with his heart, and it seems genetic. That's the message I get from Tink.

You did all that you could have done! You absolutely did the right thing by taking him to the vet when you did. You were doing what a responsible dog mum would do, and he understands that and appreciates you caring for him. You could not have known about the heart defect otherwise.

I'm getting a vision of a lot of tail wagging, and some panting. He tells me that he followed you everywhere and loved watching your feet as you padded around. He tells me about birds... he liked watching them or he's going to send you one as a message he's around.

(Photo: Tink's ready for a car ride. Credit: Michelle B.)

So, watch for any odd behavior from birds in the next week. You will hear from him!

Do you know of a brown and white dog, like a boxer or bulldog that passed before him? He's showing me that kind of dog (I don't know which it is). That dog is also around him. There's also a male figure, someone close to your age.

Tink said that he was supposed to move on when he did, and if he passed from a long sickness it would've been too much for you to bear. He is still around you, and he can hear you!

He says "please don't feel guilty. You did the right thing, mummy." There's a lot of love that binds you both together. It even looks like his little lips are formed into a smile.

I hope this helps, and please don't feel any guilt. You're a great dog mum!
Sincerely, Rob Gutro

From Michelle - Jun 8
Hello Rob, Firstly, I want to thank you, from the bottom of my heart. I truly did not expect a response from yourself with a message from Tink. You can't imagine how much comfort this has brought me, I am elated.

Secondly, you won't believe this, but it's completely true. As I read your response, the part that said to watch for a bird, well, at that exact moment... I heard a loud bang at my window. I turned to look and saw a bird flying away. That bird had flew onto my bow window and made such a noise to get my attention.

The tears rolled down my cheeks, I was astounded. I hadn't even finished reading your response and it had to be my beloved Tink.

I'm sure I will see that bird again this week. You have an amazing gift and I cannot thank you enough.

Also you were completely correct about Tink watching my feet. He would look to see what shoes I was wearing.
Trainers and he knew it was walkies. Heels and he knew I was going to work. Flats and he knew we were going out in the car.

I have a male cousin in spirit around my age and I think this is who Tink is with. The Boxer or Bulldog, I'm not sure at this point but I will ask family members.

You have given me so much hope. I feel so much calmer. Thank you Rob, You are an Angel.
Kindest Regards
Michelle

From Rob Gutro - June 8

Hi again, Michelle- Thanks for your email- I'm so pleased that Tink's messages were understood and the bird came quickly! Pets in spirit really can make things happen to assure us they are okay and are still around.

BTW, the other dog, could also be a stuffed toy that he had. I was thinking about that after I read your message. It makes sense that Tink is with your male cousin. We're all connected on this side and the other side. I'm so happy that I could provide these confirmations for you! Sending a hug, Rob

From Michelle - June 9

Hi Rob - Thank you for your email and WOW... It would be an honor for Tink's messages to appear in your new book. I can't begin to tell you how much that would mean to my family and I. Thank You.

After I read your email yesterday and after the bird banged on my window, I drove straight to my parent's house and told them what had just happened. I read them Tink's message and my mother laughed because everyone knew it was always a standing joke that Tink ALWAYS looked at what shoes I was putting on and he would act accordingly.

For example my trainers would make him run around wagging his tail excitedly as he knew it was walkies, somber, serious if it were

heels as he knew I was going to work etc... And yes he followed me EVERYWHERE... just like you said.

Also when you said his lips looked like they were in a curve as though he were smiling, this is also very true. He often looked like he was smiling. Also I am so glad he hears me as I talk to him a lot. That is a great comfort to know he hears me.

I am aware of spirits as I often get smells and I have heard them running up and down stairs etc. so I was convinced I would sense Tink too, but I haven't as yet.

Regarding the brown and white dog. I still cannot place it. I cannot think of a stuffed toy of this description and he had many toys. I will keep thinking of that and I will still ask family members. It must be relevant if he showed you this.

I feel so much better knowing he is okay and I can' thank you enough Rob. Thanks again from all of us.
Much Love, Michelle

##

Chapter 19
Scarlette and Bandit: Bandit's Spirit Appearance and a Ghost Dog Photo

In May of 2014, I received an email from Cara who asked if she could send a picture to me for explanation. I agreed, and she sent me a Polaroid holiday picture from PetSmart of her two dogs Scarlett and Bandit with Santa. What wasn't expected is that there appeared to be a third dog in the photo! To the right of "Santa" there was what appeared to be the ghost of a dog that looked like a West Highland Terrier.

As ghost investigators know, sometimes Earth-bound ghosts or spirits (that crossed over) will appear in photos so this is nothing new, but it is unusual.

What's even more interesting is that Cara did not recognize the dog. In addition to the mysterious ghost dog in the photo, Cara also explained about how her sister's dog, Bandit made physical appearances after his passing. Following are Cara's emails to me and the photo:

From Cara - May 14
In 2006- My twin sister lived with me at the time and we both have Pekingese/Maltese mix dogs. I have the sister named Scarlette age 5 (age15 now) and my twin had the brother named Bandit.

Bandit passed during a Myelogram at the Emergency Vet on 2/14/06 age 5 unexpectedly. The weekend before he passed away, he was at the emergency vet awaiting a specialist to come in that following Monday.

I woke up out of my sleep in my bed and saw a little girl in a white robe smiling- it was like a vision (film strip on my wall?) and in the most vibrant color I ever saw. Like Technicolor back in the movies in 1950's. I said hello, and she turned like she was looking at something that I could not see, and faded away.

I told my twin about it and later realized she was greeting Bandit after he passed. Well he passed away a few days later, when we got his ashes, my dad was visiting and saw a black animal run down the hall. He asked me why my black cat was in the house. I told him he never comes in the house. Nothing more thought about it, then my son that was 15 at the time saw a black dog run through the back yard, late afternoon about dark I have a fenced in yard, no other animals were in my yard. It was Bandit.

Then my twin sister and I started experiencing something jumping on our bed on separate occasions walk up and curl up at our feet. Look and nothing be there.

My dog was at the Vet for kidney stones at the time and I felt it the morning I was getting up to get ready to go pick her up. Then my twin had an out body dream and sat up out of her body on the living room floor, sleeping on a blow up mattress, because the room she stayed in was being remodeled. She said the room turned white and Bandit jumped in her lap wagging his tail she said she felt the most incredible peace come over her. She petted him and he appeared to be around one year old. She told him she loved him then he ran to a bowl of water drank some, and then ran off and disappeared. She woke up sitting up. Ran and woke me up to tell me about it.

One and one half months later I rescued a Pekingese from Atlanta Humane Society and we brought him home and was feeling very guilty about it.

That next morning I woke up on the mattress on the living room floor. I let Carla slept in my bed in my bedroom that night and Scarlette was lying beside me. She barked the weirdest bark once, like a howl type bark and I looked and there was Bandit on the back patio walking by. I went and looked out and he was gone.

Enclosed is a picture of Bandit a few months before he got sick and passed, he is the black and white Peke mix, Look above his head? We did not notice this until after he passed. Looks like a ghost dog? We have the other picture taken before this one that shows the white dog mist forming?

Scarlette is the Blonde and white Peke Mix, she is now 15 years old.

From Rob Gutro - May 17

Hi Cara - Thank you for sharing these incredible stories. It seems that Bandit has a strong spirit and keeps coming back to you, your twin, your son and even your dad. Wow. That's a lot of spirit activity- and such a testament to the incredible bond you share.

The jumping on the bed and curling up sounds more like the spirit of a cat to me. Many people I've talked with said their cats used to do that in life and continued to do that in the afterlife.

The photo certainly looks like a white dog, like a white terrier to the immediate right of Santa. Did you have a white terrier? Like a highland terrier?
Rob Gutro - Ghosts and Spirits

From Cara - May 18

We didn't have that kind of dog, but Bandit and Scarlette's dad was a Maltese. You're very welcome to use our story. My twin sister and I never experienced anything like it before.

(Photo: Bandit, spirit dog, Santa and Scarlett. Credit: Cara)

Conclusions and Possibilities

It's difficult to know who the mysterious spirit or ghost dog is in the photo. There are several possibilities. The dog could be associated with Cara's childhood, or a dog connected one of her relatives or friends. On the other hand, the dog could be connected to someone who was in the store at the time, or even connected to "Santa."

##

Chapter 20
Pierre Ensures the Message Comes Through

In June, 2015 I happened to be on Facebook and saw a posting from one of the dog rescues that I work with. The posting was about a black poodle named Pierre and I knew I was led to it.

Pierre was the childhood black poodle of my friend Maureen in Massachusetts, who passed in the 1980s (before I knew Maureen). Pierre first revealed himself to me when came through to me in 2014. At that time, Maureen's dad was slowly failing in the hospital. His message was that he would be waiting for Maureen's dad on the other side, next to Maureen's mom who passed in 1989.

So, Pierre came back again to me on what turned out to be the same day that Maureen was thinking about him. Maureen lives 400 miles away from me, so there was no way I could have known she was thinking about Pierre that morning.

Pierre's Message to Me
My friend Janet's Facebook posting from the Dachshund rescue she works with said, "And [here's a photo of] our "ugly dachshund," Pierre the poodle, with his new mom and dad!
I immediately knew that I was drawn to that posting and the photo of a black poodle named Pierre, because it was a message for my friend Maureen.

From Rob:
YOU just got a message from Pierre. I was thinking about you, and this dog adoption (from the Dachshund rescue of all places) popped up, citing a successful adoption of a black poodle... named Pierre. Pierre was making me think of you today, and then he told me he wants to let you know that he's around you. He says that you should watch Lily, because she will see him today. How cool! Rob

(Photo: a Pierre doppelganger)

From Maureen:

Wow!!!!! So funny that you tell me this today because I was just thinking about Pierre on my morning walk with Lily today. Thinking about how important he was to my mom like [my dog] Lily is to me [now]. Pierre was the same way with my mom. My mother took it so hard when my dad had to put Pierre down. It was her baby. They had the same relationship. Maureen

There's no such thing as a coincidence when spirit is involved. Spirits can also be persistent when they want you to know they're around. Pierre influenced Maureen to think of him on her morning walk so she would know he's still around. Pierre then used me to confirm it. He led me to find a photo of the same dog breed, same color and even the same name (on the photo)! He knew I would understand the message was for Maureen and share it to confirm he's still around her decades later. .

##

Chapter 21
Aggy Tells Me She's a Dog and Gives the Perfect Description

I received a plea for help on Facebook messenger about a woman named Cheryl, whose pet had passed. Cheryl was so deep in grief she didn't say if her pet was a dog or a cat and didn't tell me anything about their size or coloring.

As I learned from spirit, her pet is a dog who came through to me with an indication of who she was with and described to me what she looked like. It's amazing how our pets can convey this information. Following is the email conversation:

From Cheryl - July 1
Hi Rob, We just got done watching your video on "Do animals go to heaven, and do they have souls." Well we recently had to let my Aggy girl go and I was wondering if you could tell if she is with my family that has passed on, and will she come to visit me. We miss her very much, but I know she is in a better place now. Could you please help us? Thank you

From Rob Gutro - July 5
Hi Cheryl - So sorry about your loss. Yes, animals do cross over and go to "heaven," "paradise" or however you wish to think of the other side! - And I'm getting the sense that Aggy was welcomed with open arms - Did your mother pass? I see a woman on the other side with literally, arms opened, who is older than you and I get a sense of mothering. Also, she's patting you on the back, assuring that Aggy is safe. "You worry so much," she said. There's no need for the worry - they're together. You have quite a number of people on the other side, too.

I'm also seeing a whitish-colored dog, with medium fur. Do you know that dog? -There's a dark area on the muzzle, too. Almost like the colorations in an Australian shepherd.

I also understand that sunrise is a time you take note that Aggy isn't around anymore. Is there something special about sunrises?
Rob

From Cheryl - July 7
Hi Rob - thank for letting me know Aggy is with my Mom who passed in 2008. You also said your see a whitish dog with a dark muzzle, well Aggy was white and with a dark muzzle.

And it's true about sunrise. Since her passing I've been up early and watching the sunrise. Wow I am thankful for your news and we stay in touch. I'm still having a hard time with her passing, but I know she is in a better place and loved as much as I did. Thank you again.

Can I see Aggy again - like you said on a video that you saw your dog in real life - but it was a ghost?
Will I be able to see Aggy walk around my house as a ghost and will I get messages from her? Please reply. Thank you.

From Rob Gutro -
Hi Cheryl- You may see Aggy, but most likely, you'll see Aggy in a dream - that's the easiest way for spirits to visit. I've only seen a few spirits - mostly they show me what they look like in my mind. That's how I saw Aggy!

In fact, I didn't know what Aggy looked like-so I'm glad I got to see her in my mind. She is so strongly connected to you. - Before you go to sleep ask her to come in your dreams. She will. You may also hear her walk around the house from time to time, protecting you.
BTW- I had no idea if Aggy was a dog or cat when you wrote me! - This is a good example of how pets show mediums what they look

like (her colors). I'm always amazed at how much information they provide!! Just know that she's around you from time to time!

(Photo: Aggy in her pajamas. Credit: Cindy P.)

From Cheryl - July 15

Rob - I just wanted to say thank you for all you've done and telling me that he is okay. It really means a lot to me that you that you did and I just want to say thank you.

I have one more question for you - If I get another Chihuahua will Aggie be mad at me and think that I betrayed her? Please respond as soon as you can thank you and thank you for all you've done.

From Rob Gutro - Jul 19

Hi Cheryl- Aggy would be happy if you bring in another dog to the family. However, she'd like you not to use her bowl! That's funny.

Seems like she was protective of her food... or at least her dish. - Once our dogs pass, they usually want us to adopt another and save a dog's life and give another dog a chance at the love they experienced with the pet parent!

So, yes, adopt another dog... Just know that Aggy may help you choose which dog, and when the dog comes into your house, he or she will be able to see Aggy from time to time, as Aggy will be helping teach the new dog how to behave in the home!

##

Chapter 22
Chloe's Comfort

This chapter contains several emails from an exchange I had with a woman named Sheila in March 2015 over the loss of her beloved dog, Chloe. Chloe provided me with two very specific signs. One to confirm her identity to me and her mom and another as a sign she's around.

From Sheila - Mar 16, 2015
Hi Rob, I attended the speaking event you had at Barron's Store last year and I'm sorry I cannot remember the date. I know you meet a lot of people and not sure if you remember me. I came up to buy 2 of your books and became extremely emotional telling you about my dog Chloe that passed away suddenly on May 9, 2013 while at the Emergency Vet.

I remember you telling us that grief will block them from connecting with us after death. I am still so very grief stricken of losing her to this day. It actually feels like my heart is still broken into a thousand pieces. You told me to send you an email to see if perhaps you could make a connection with her. I just felt brave enough to ask you in hopes you may be able to tell me some kind of message from her.

I have 2 other dogs that have passed on, they were 15 and 12 years old. Chloe was just a month shy of turning 8 years old. She was a very nervous girl but when she fell ill that night I never dreamed she would die and it kills me that they made me leave her. I was gone maybe 1 hour when they called me to say she passed away, I should have been there.

My other dogs I was able to seek peace in their passing even though I had to make the heart wrenching decision to have them put down within 9 months of the other. I felt their presence here at home and I dreamt of them. I can't even dream of Chloe and I thought I felt her at my felt one night when I was very sick with a migraine but wasn't for sure as I was very ill that night and on pain meds. I have another dog Maggie, who has seen me through my heartache and I love her. I just can't seem to get passed losing Chloe, it becomes so overwhelming at times.

(Photo: Chloe. Credit: Sheila B.)

Anyway, I just thought I would finally reach out to you and just see what happens. I thank you for your time in reading my email and if you get any messages from other loved ones please tell me. I think you are an amazing person and I enjoyed your books and the talk you gave at Barron's. I hope to see you again in the near future.
Sheila

From Rob Gutro - Mar 16, 2015

Hi Sheila- Thank you for your email. I'm so sorry that you're still struggling with Chloe's passing. There's scientific studies that prove that we grieve more for our pet children than we do for human relatives, so it's a natural thing.

Yes, your grief is likely blocking your ability to receive her messages, although it sounds like you did get a physical confirmation she was around you.

She, like your other two dogs that have passed won't be around you all the time. Just every now and then. You'll especially sense them when you're worn out emotionally or tired, or not feeling well. Why? Because dogs on this side and the other side always want to comfort us.

When I read your email, I kept getting sense of a heart ailment - something to do with the heart. Did Chloe have a heart issue that led to breathing difficulties?

One thing I do know, is that Chloe does not want you to carry guilt around because you were told to leave her at the emergency vet. She is bound to you by love. She knew you were taking her there to help her. On the other side, she knows what you did and she read your emotions when you were taking her there. You need to let the guilt go - it's unhealthy and she doesn't want you to continue feeling that way. There's no need for it.

Something I mention often is that people and dogs and cats choose how they want to pass. Some prefer to pass at home surrounded by family or friends. Others want to transition privately. My mom passed in Dec. 2013, and waited until me and my husband arrived in her hospital room (she was unresponsive but I know her spirit heard me), and she waited until we and my brothers all left for the night. It was after we all left that she passed. That was the case with Chloe.

In addition, your other two dogs were waiting for her to take her across and into the light. She's also with other members of your human family.

When you see your first yellow flower of the season - around your house- either outside or inside, and it doesn't need to be an actual flower, it can be a picture, know that Chloe is there with you. That's a sign you can look for. In fact, after you see the first yellow flower, Chloe would like you to get a bouquet of yellow flowers for yourself and remember that she's with you.

I hope that this helps you. Just know she's around you from time to time. I hope you find comfort in this email and feel free to write me back. -Rob

From Sheila - March 21, 2015
Hi Rob, Thank you your response! I just got your email today it was delivered into SPAM and I have been checking from my phone and just thought you hadn't had a chance to write me back yet.

I got on my desk top and looked into SPAM mail and there was your response. I'm taken aback by your response because you are correct on the breathing difficulties with Chloe. She was a very high strung nervous dog that I had been giving Xanax to calm her for the last 3 years of her life. She began with what were like panic attacks that lead to her literally gasping for breath and she would jump onto my chest sometimes in the middle of the night.

It was hard to take her to the vet as she would go into these panic fits and had an extreme one when I took her for thyroid tests one day. They had to sedate her and almost intubate her.

My vet had her on meds to help with the throat spasms but it seemed to make matters worse and I stopped it. She was very clingy to me from the day I brought her home and I loved it. I held her all the time and carried her whenever she wanted me to. She was spoiled rotten.

The night she passed away it came on suddenly just like the other attacks and she knew that I made her better with the medication because she kept accepting it and taking it. She began salivating really bad and at that point I knew I had to get her help. I really just thought they would give her something stronger to calm her down and we would come home in a few hours.

When we got there she of course got more anxious and they took her back where they came and told me her chest was full of fluid. They tapped her and could not get the fluid off of her chest and explained to me if they got her stable would I take her to see vet cardiologist as it appeared she was in congestive heart failure.

I heard her let out 1 cry and told them she wouldn't settle down unless I held her, with that they gave her to me and she went limp in my arms. I sat with her in an oxygen crate for hours and finally they told me to go home and come back in couple hours.

I have struggled with this because of the way it happened so quick and thought they let her die and if I could have done something different or faster. All the things I know everyone else thinks when something like this happens.

I was with my 90 year-old grandmother when she passed away and I guess being with my other dogs when they passed I just couldn't let go of the fact they told me to leave. Her being only almost 8 years old was another issue for me.

You have made me feel better as far as her condition and that I know it was her time to go. She completed her job here with me and she was done and knew me well enough she did not want me to see her pass.

I take comfort in knowing she is with Max, Molly and my family that is on the other side, I was worried she would be scared and not know anyone. I'm so glad to know they came for her to help her cross over, I can so see them doing that for me.

Chloe came into my life and got me through hard times and 2 of which was losing them just 9 months apart. My Maggie came in a crazy well as well just 2 days after Chloe's passing and I felt extreme guilt for that which made Maggie quite the challenge in the beginning due to my grief for Chloe.

Turns out she is quite a character and I believe Chloe sent her my way to keep me going because I literally thought I would die without her.

I have to tell you, as I was typing the first email to you I have a picture of her in a frame with yellow daffodils setting by the computer. Amazing!

I will be looking for those yellow flowers and will get a bouquet of yellow flowers in her honor. Thank you so much!

I will definitely contact Carol and see if I can sit in on your talk. Thanks again so very much for responding to me and it does give me comfort in knowing what you've told me. You are awesome Rob and I feel honored to have met you and for you to share your gift with me. I just can't thank you enough!!!! Sheila :)

From Rob Gutro -Mar 21, 2015

Hi Sheila - I'm so pleased that Chloe's messages to me made sense to you.

The heart failure and the yellow flowers were specific signs she gave me to identify her to you. I hope you know now that Chloe does not want you to feel any guilt. She wanted to pass on her own accord.

I'm so excited that these messages were so specific and understandable, and that you know that Chloe is around you all from time to time. Rob Gutro

From Sheila March 22, 2015

Hi Rob, You have to know, I feel a sense of peace ever since I got your email. I am still missing her terribly and have had still emotional break downs but in a better way if that makes sense.

She was such a sweet silly little soul and it has truly been hard to lose her. I feel like she held on honestly until she couldn't no more. The last 3 years of her life, now when I think back, were hard on her with the anxiety. I just went along with it and would have been just as happy to take care of her another 10 years just like she was if I could have. She couldn't even bear for me to leave the house even with my husband here. He would often, the last year have to call me home as he couldn't get her settled down and would be afraid of her breathing. I've loved all my dogs and dealt with lots of health issues and I'm doing it again with Maggie and will probably do it after her. I love them so much.

I attached 3 pictures of her. She was so beautiful I just couldn't get enough pictures of her. Again, thanks so much you are truly an inspiration and wonderful person. Sheila :)

##

Chapter 23
Phinn's Musical Message

Music is a powerful way to send a message to someone from spirit. As I mentioned in Chapter 4, we often hear songs that make us think of a loved one that passed, or realize a special connection that the person or pet in spirit has to the song.

When my dog Buzz passed, the first song I heard was Garth Brooks' song "The Dance," about a man who was grateful for the short time he had with someone he loved. Although that song was over a decade old and now two decades old, sometimes when I'm thinking of Buzz, the song will come on.

In this chapter you'll read about a dog mom who wrote me for a sign and her dog Phinn provided a special musical one.

For those who are skeptical, please keep in mind that I receive emails from people whom I don't know anything about - I don't know where they live, what music they like, what they do for a living, etc. So, when a pet sends a musical message and the pet parent understands it, that's confirmation that it is their pet communicating.

From Tina - Sept. 27, 2014
I just finished reading "Pets and the Afterlife." Thank you so much for writing it! I have found comfort and your words (and the stories of others) have helped me to grieve a little less. Phinn was a pug/dachshund mix. He suffered in his last days of life. He was very sick with pancreatitis. Ending his suffering was like ripping out my heart.

I just want a sign that he is OK now. I want to know if he's upset because Chico (my daughter's Chihuahua who lives with me) is still here - they didn't have the best of relationships. I have his ashes near me and wear a locket ring that has 2 of his little baby teeth in it. Every night I ask him to come visit, but, I've not seen him yet. I thought one night I may have felt him lying next to me, but, I'm not sure. Am I trying too hard? Is my grief still too bad? I feel like I didn't give him enough attention after Chico came to live with us. My heart aches.

Is there anything else I can do but wait? Can you help me? Anything you might can tell me would be so greatly appreciated. Thank you, Rob, for reading this.
Bright Blessings ~ Tina

From Rob Gutro

Hi Tina- I just finished reading your email and over the internet came a song for you from Phinn! "I Will Always Love You" by Dolly Parton. It's still playing as I write. It's Phinn's message to you. There are no such things as coincidences, which is why the song came on as I was answering your email.

Phinn inspired me to start reading your email when that song came on so you could know the message of love was for you. It was his time to go, but the love he shares will always be with you. - I'm actually sitting here in tears writing this.

Please listen to the ENTIRE song. Here's a link to the video: https://www.youtube.com/watch?v=6j4U66RYzQo

He doesn't want you to grieve anymore. Instead he wants you to celebrate the love you shared. Remember the times together and talk with him out loud! He can hear you!

Yes, you did feel him. You tried to explain it away, but it was him. Thank you for letting me know you enjoyed the book. This has been a VERY emotional reading for me.

To honor him, he says "when you're ready mommy" - please save another doggy and give them the love you gave me. I'll be there helping train him or her, and I'll even help you pick him out.

Rob Gutro

##

Part 3:
Messages from Pets to Their Parents

This part of the book contains stories that pet parents shared with me about how they have recognized signs from their dogs or cats. They've graciously allowed me to share their experiences.

Because our pets communicate with us in so many ways, it is important to include stories that provide many different examples, as your pets may use the same or similar methods.

###

Chapter 24
Dali's Rainbow and Chimes

The following story was graciously provided by Dorothy, mom to Dali, a Lhasa Apso. Dali provided several signs that she was still around after her physical passing.

From Dorothy - Oct 28

I just finished reading your book and it gave me a lot of comfort to know my pet is still here. I lost my Lhasa Apso (12 1/2) on Sept 27, 2014.

I am older and she is my whole life, my soulmate, my best friend. She got sick quickly and went to the vet on a Friday (who said she would be fine, gave prescription) and she died the next morning very quickly and unexpectedly. I am devastated.

The next morning I was trying to cope and went outside the front door and a beautiful rainbow was there. It had not been raining, but the rainbow was gorgeous and directly over my house. I cried and cried and immediately went inside and googled "rainbows." I was directed to the Rainbows Bridge website (had never heard of it) and it became my outlet over the last month. I related the rainbow story and someone suggested your book. I immediately ordered it and read it, great insight.

I know the rainbow was a gift from my Dali. A few days later one of my wind chimes sang when I was outside. NO wind and only one of them. I looked up and felt my Dali. I have never been one to

121

believe in all of these things, but I know now they are real. It gives me great comfort to know I will again be with my beloved Dali.

(Photo: Dali. Credit: Dorothy)

I would be honored for you to share Dali's story. Dali is my life and I want everyone to know about her. Thank you so much.

Two weeks ago we had a tornado in town. I was with a group of people who were "herded" to a safer place inside a store. Everyone was upset, very worried, on cells, etc. For some reason I was extremely calm, more so than ever before. I knew I would be okay, Dali was there. Or maybe it was time to go to where she was?

I will never fear death now and look forward to the light. All of this has changed me totally into a different person. I see the good now... thank you, Dali.

And I just wanted to thank you for your book, it helped me more than you know.
God Bless, Dorothy

From Rob Gutro

Hi Dorothy- I am so glad that you recognized the signs from Dali- the rainbow is an amazing sign, and she was with you during the tornado! Dogs become our guardians on the other side.

I am so elated that you found comfort in the book but more so in the signs that you've already received.

Thank you for sharing, and my deepest sympathy on her physical loss- but grateful to hear of her spirit around you! Rob Gutro

##

Chapter 25
2 Sets of Paw Prints from the Heart

Dogs and cats can leave physical signs that they're still around you. In the following two stories that were shared with me, Savannah Lynn and Tenshi let their pet parents know that they're still around with paw prints!

Paw Prints on a New Rug - From Barbara W.

My chi, Savannah Lynn passed away after 25 years with me & shortly afterward I was sitting in the bathtub crying (my nightly ritual) & when I looked down at my bath mat there where paw prints imbedded in it (it had just been put down that day) as if she had been standing there ~~ she used to lay beside the tub on the mat every single night!

Even in the end when she was so sick, she would drag herself into the bathroom while I bathed.

~~ I know her spirit visits me just like my mother's spirit does at times ~~ I would be very interested in reading about experiences others have had! I know how comforting mine have been for me.

##

Tenshi's Paw Print - From Pat

Hi Rob, I just listened to your show on YouTube, paranormal review radio. I wanted to send you this picture.

I just lost my big, beautiful Akita in a totally unexpected and untimely way. An infection was brewing in his body and it hit like a time bomb last Thursday evening, and within three days he was gone. We took him to emergency twice on Sunday and that's where I left him on IV and heavily drugged.

(Photo: Tenshi. Credit: Pat)

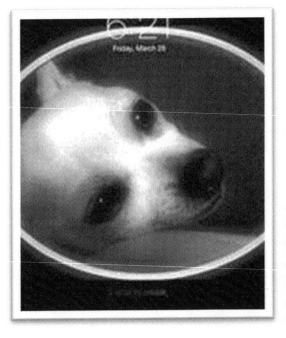

Monday, when I woke up, I got the bad news. When I was getting ready to go pick up his body (trying to hold it together), I wet my shirt on the bathroom counter. When I backed up, this is what I saw.

I walked Tenshi (angel in Japanese) like crazy, and fed, and took care of him the best I could trying to prolong his life. He went everywhere with me. He was such a good man and the closest thing I had to a child. He had poor teeth due to hereditary. He was otherwise healthy. It's all I can come up with. He just turned 8. Thank you Rob. - Pat

From Rob Gutro

Pat my deepest sympathies on the passing on Tenshi. What an amazing sign from him in the shape of a paw print on your shirt. That was his way of letting you know that he's okay and still around.

He can hear you, too, so know that you can talk with him. He passed quickly to prevent you from having to make the decision. He's pain free with wagging tail. I'm seeing a brown and white rope like object, perhaps a toy. He wants you to keep that with his ashes. Put up a photo of him next to it and talk with him every morning as you did when he was here.

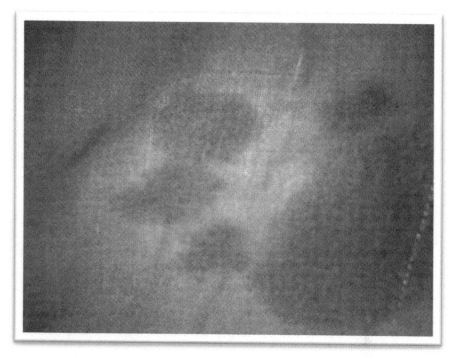

(Photo: Tenshi's paw print on Pat's shirt. Credit: Pat)

The bond is strong. Did you adopt him when he was young? I'm getting the sense of a good part of his life with you. You were actually drawn together by a woman on the other side. Does any of this make sense to you? - Rob

From Pat

The way it happened so quickly and as large as he was, I buried him up on a mountain in a beautiful spot unable to make preparations for a cremation.

This last Sunday, I was finally able (emotionally) to go up there to pretty his grave up with beach rocks and top soil. I'll plant bulbs in the fall and I have to think about a marker. My friend snipped some of his soft hair from behind his ear which I have in a small bottle. That's all I have of him. I've created a little shrine in my room with his hair in the bottle and his picture.

As far as you saying that you sensed a good part of his life with me. I watched his Mother give birth to his litter, and I took him home at six weeks. I always felt good about the fact that he was one of the fortunate ones who was never orphaned and never would be. It's possible that a woman brought us together, but I can't think of who that might be.

He has a tiny brown and white bunny toy which I let the old man I'm a live-in caregiver for keep in his room. I'm not going to take it back, and besides, I think Tenshi wouldn't mind him having it. They were extremely fond of each other. I do talk to him constantly. Thank you Rob for your response and take care.

##

Chapter 26
Mary's Cat and Horse Spirit Experiences

From Mary - March 29

Hi Rob, Just wanted to let you know how much I enjoyed your book on animal visitations. Got it Thursday evening and finished it Friday. It was great, thank you for writing it, I know it will bring comfort to a lot of people who have pets that have crossed over or who know that is something that they will one day have to face.

In my 60 years on this plane I have been blessed to have known and cared for 17 fur kids. All of them were rescues in one way or another, and all of them blessed me with unconditional love and support. When it seemed like all else had failed me or would fail me, they never did.

For much of this time, if any of the fur kids came back, I was unaware of it. I consider myself a healer rather than a medium, although with the Reiki that I practice some "sight" is always tossed into the mix because we work in sacred space on the spiritual, emotional and physical planes all at the same time to help someone facilitate their healing - there is a huge dose of Spirit in everything we do.

Starting 15 years ago, when I started working with Reiki I did notice the occasional visit.

I had to make "that decision" for one of the cats shortly after I was attuned to Reiki. He had had a number of debilitating chronic conditions since birth and at the age of 13 finally let me know it was "time." About a week or 10 days after Peanut passed I was attending the funeral of my partner's Grandmother.

For a number of reasons I was not allowed to sit with the family, so I was off to one side in a pew and started to meditate when Peanut crawled up from my lap onto my shoulder and started to knead my shoulder and hair. He had come to me as an 11 day old cast-off kitten, eyes not fully open.

I had to nurse him with a bottle for several months and for night nursing he was so tiny (hence the name Peanut) he would sleep in the hollow of my collar bone and it was a habit he never got over, even when he was a full grown 14 pound cat and not only covered the hollow of my collarbone but my throat and half of my face!

There was no mistaking it was Peanut and that he was letting me know I had done the right thing and that he was pain free, happy and waiting for me. I had felt guilty about Peanut, not in that it was his time, but about whether I had done all I could for him with all of his physical problems. This was his way of putting my mind at ease.

Since then I have only had 2 other occurrences where pets have come through to me. When my last relationship (human to human) dissolved, I unexpectedly inherited my Ex's 2 cats. We had shared our lives with 9 cats over the years and at the dissolution of our relationship we still had 6 of them with us.

Stasia had been with L since he was a kitten, before and during our relationship and then I had him for another 3 1/2 years after we split. Stasia had a VERY strong personality and he made his likes, dislikes and presence known where ever he went. He also assumed that it was his responsibility to rule over the other 8 cats in our clowder.

Well, back to the point of this. One of his favorite things to do, and one that annoyed me the most, was to walk figure 8's around my feet when I was working in the kitchen. He would do this, I would holler, shove him out of the room and he would stalk the doorways waiting for me to forget he was there so he could sneak in and do it again!!

Well, for 4-8 weeks after he passed, at least 2-3 times a week I would feel him brushing against my legs, wrapping his long bushy tail around my ankles and trying to trip me in the kitchen. This was the period when my grief was at its peak and hardest for me to manage. He knew I was lonely, missing him and need reassurance. While I still miss him dearly, he seems to know that I no longer need the reassurance and he has contented himself with the rare appearance in the background of a dream now and then or on rare occasions I will see him from the corner of my eye just for a second.

A Message from a Horse

For 20 years I shared my life with my registered quarter horse named Roany Mac. Mac was another rescue who took a lot of patience and perseverance to bring around (and more than one visit to the emergency room on my part).

But he paid back the time and patience in spades by giving the BEST hugs ever, listening to all of my problems and joys, sharing glorious spring days riding in the Adirondack foothills and even letting me soak his shoulder with my tears when my marriage broke up. He, and Beggar (my 25 pound tomcat) were besties and were also my best friends during their lives with me.

His end was swift and devastating. On rare occasions, a horse can, while rolling on the ground, cause a loop of the bowel to twist on itself and cut of the blood flow to the tissues. This is called a torsion colic and unless it is caught immediately and corrected surgically it is always lethal. This is what had happened to Mac.

I came home from work and he didn't greet me - Rain, shine snow, sleet, hail, tornado, that fool would always stand and knicker to me *when I came in the driveway. I checked on him, found him in severe distress, did a physical exam and called the vet.*

The gist was - torsion colic, profound shock and irreversible organ failure. It had probably occurred that morning right after I left for work. The worst news was that the vet was 2 hours away and Mac would be in unbearable agony for that time if I waited for the vet to put him down. I decided not to wait and put him down myself. Yep, the grief and guilt were staggering and I have spent 17 years missing him.

Anyway, not a word from him for those 17 years. Then, when I was at Nancy's house for meditation group one night, I kept feeling like someone was standing behind me rubbing the top of my head and pulling on my hair, blowing hot breath on the top of my head. Weirdest of all, it was comforting rather than spooky.

After the meditation when we were talking about anything that had come through for any of the group Nancy said she could see a big dark horse standing behind me, he had a white stripe down his nose and a small white mark between his nostrils and he kept messing with my hair. Well, Nancy has never seen a picture of Mac and I have never described him to her, or even talked about him, but she got him to a T, and one of his favorite things to do to me was to come up behind me and grab my ponytail and pull on it with his lips or rub his lips on the top of my head and blow at me!! No doubt at all that it was him playing with my hair for over 20-30 minutes during and after the meditation.

I have now read and thoroughly enjoyed all 3 of your books. I know they are doing good, dispelling many of the fallacies about "the sight" and Spirit. I am glad we have had the chance to meet. -Mary

##

Chapter 27
Mikie the Cat Leads and Shows a Double

This is a story about how a cat's spirit led her "dad" to her remains hidden outside, and brought a doppelganger kitty to his attention, to let him know she was still with him. Spirits will guide us to places and will show us pets (or people) that resemble them, to let us know that they're still with us from time to time.

The other lesson in this story is that the spirit of our pets who have passed come back and teach our new pets the same behaviors and same habits. That's exactly what Mikie's spirit did with the new cat, Michi.

I met Robbie, an events photographer, at one of the events I attended. Robbie works at Bayline Studios Photography in Reisterstown, Maryland. He shared an amazing story. Here's his Facebook page: www.facebook.com/baylinestudiosphotography.

Robbie said: *My first cat was named Mikie because I did not know she was a female (a Michelle). I got Mikie from one of my newspaper route customers, Mrs. Kaufman. Because she did not have the money for the collections I was doing that week, she asked if I would take a kitten instead. I said sure. Put this tiny little fuzzball in my delivery bag and went on to finish the last couple of houses.*

My folks were leaving on vacation with a group of friends that night and my grandparents were staying with us. So, I figured there was no way they could tell me not to keep the cat. From that night, Mikie and I forged a very unique bond. I was 10 at the time, and Mikie would be with me until after college.

She would always greet me at the door, would always jump on my lap then right shoulder. No matter how long I was away, she always came running when she heard my car door close. We both began to get older and Mikie had begun to have some mobility and health issues. She was over 100 in people years.

One day she gave me her usual head butt and waddled off into the yard. I did not see her for a couple of days, then a week then two. I had a very weird feeling that she had said goodbye to me in her own way. Then about a month later I was doing some yard work for my mom, cleaning out the pachysandra [ground cover] where Mikie used to like to lie in the shade on hot summer days, when I came across something metallic. It was her name tag and collar next to a little skeleton. I was oddly OK with it as I know she led me there to find it. I still have her tag.

Mikie Sends a Doppelganger

Fast forward about 30 years. Another little critter comes into my life. The resemblance to Mikie is striking.

A friend asked if we would like a kitten, and I said sure, but this time I remembered that my wife is allergic to cats, so I said "on a trial basis." I put my head down in front of the kitten, to see what she would do. Instant head butt and purring. Then I picked her up and try to put her on my left shoulder. She wanted nothing to do with it and scrambled to my right and nudged up to me, just like Mikie. Then my wife got home and I expected a sneezing fit. Nothing. We decided to see how it goes.

As the days went on our new kitty, named Michi (friend in Italian) is showing behavior, mannerisms and speech patterns, just like Mikie. The resemblance is unreal, the temperament is unreal. She sits in the same places as Mikie used to, she sleeps with me just like Mikie used to. She is just so cool to have around. My wife is still allergic to cats... just not this one!

##

Chapter 28
Spirit Dog Revives Her Dad

Cleopatra was a Great Dane that lived in a happy home from 2001 to her passing in 2006. In her five short years on Earth in the physical she developed a deep bond of love that was so powerful it helped her save the life of her dad from the other side.

The following story was graciously provided from Ron and Shirley W., as proof of how our pets can do amazing things even in spirit, and that the love we share with them binds us to them. Ron describes how Cleo visited him and revived him.

Ron wrote: *Our son purchased Cleo as a puppy while he lived in Maryland and attended college at George Washington University. Once our son graduated he moved back to New York with Cleo. They both moved in with us for a short time.*

Cleo was the kind of dog that anyone could love once you met her. Although a large dog, most of the time she thought she was a lap dog! She had a habit of climbing up on my recliner to sit on my lap.

She also loved to dance with you as well. Now just think, a dog that stood over six foot while on her back legs...paws on your shoulders... dancing! It was a site to behold. Cleo would run in circles like a grey hound chasing a rabbit. While she was alive all of us just loved her. Sadly, at 5 years of age, Cleo was diagnosed with a cancer that was wrapped around her spine. Soon after she was diagnosed we lost her.

We all missed Cleo since her passing. We could not understand why we lost her so soon. A year later I came to understand why.

(Photo: Ron and Shirley's grandson with Cleo. Credit: RW)

I had become ill, but like many of us, I kept pushing on to keep up with my busy life and responsibilities. My illness started with just a sore throat. After a couple of weeks dealing with the sore throat, my tonsils had gotten abscessed and breathing had become difficult.

One afternoon I sat in my recliner to rest while my wife was on the couch keeping an eye on me since it was not like me to want to sleep in the middle of the day.

I remember taking the nap, but the strangest thing was that I felt really at ease and in a very good place. It is hard to explain the nap except that I felt care free from all pressures of life. That is when I saw Cleo again. Cleo wanted me to play with her and I did. After a while we sat down to rest.

During the visit, I sat in my recliner and Cleo sat alongside me; I was petting her, thinking how much I missed her. Cleo started to lick me on my face. That was when I actually started to wake up and regain consciousness.

As I became aware of my surroundings, I realized my wife was at my side shaking and trying to wake me. She said that I had stopped breathing and she was trying to get me to respond and start breathing!

Once I was fully awake, the first thing I told her was I had seen Cleo, played with her and woke up when Cleo started to lick my face.

Once I realized what happened, I told my wife I better go to the emergency room and have this taken care of since I was having trouble breathing. My wife said she thought Cleo came to me in order to save my life.

One could say it was a dream. I do have dreams but nothing as real and as peaceful as when I was with Cleo. She has never been in a dream after that day but has always been in my prayers and thoughts.

I truly believed that I had died that day and it was not a dream when I was with Cleo. I realized she was letting me know it was not my time and her sprit was with me and watching over me.

We have had many pets over the years. Never before nor since this one episode has this happened to me. We give love to our pets and in times of grave need, they come to our rescue.

##

Chapter 29
A Good Morning Meow and Movement

The following email came to me from a friend who has two senior dogs and read "Pets and the Afterlife (1)." It's interesting how spirit works. You'll see how the spirit of a cat can influence someone to go to a place where they can get comfort.

From Keith: I bought your new book Pets and the Afterlife, knowing that it would be the most difficult of the three for me to read. I love our pets more than is probably usual and, after losing our 11-year-old beagle Naismith in December of 2012, I've been in a bit of a rut. To add to it, his twin brother, Everett, who is now 13, has slowed down quite a bit and I often worry about the day we'll have to say goodbye to him.

But that's not why I'm writing. I wanted to tell you that as soon as I got the book in the mail, I tore through it and was about 3/4 of the way done with it when Eric and I hosted a little happy-hour/get-together with some people in our new building.

One friend in particular, Lynn, who lives on the 3rd floor of our building (and who LOVES Everett) seemed a little "out of sorts" that afternoon. Lynn is retired and is one of those great people that seems to spread happiness wherever she goes. But this day, I could tell there was something on her mind. In the middle of the party, I asked her how things were and she shared with me that her cat, Gideon, had passed away 2 days earlier. Fighting tears, she shared how awful it was to find him lifeless in her condo and how she picked him up, cried, and ran downstairs for help.

She went on to tell me that, since that day, Lynn had experienced some very unusual feelings. She said that, the night before, she laid down to go to bed and sensed that Gideon was with her. She said she even felt the weight of his presence (he was a large cat) next to her where he always slept. The next morning, she said that she could swear that she was awakened by the sound of Gideon's meow. He always woke her up with a loud "good morning" meow and she said she was a bit scared because she really believes she heard it again that morning.

I was heart-broken to hear about Lynn's loss so, before she left the party, I asked her to come to the back of our condo with me- I told her I had something I wanted to show her. I let her know that some of the things she was sharing with me seemed to come right out of your book. I told her I was reading about the signs our pets give us and that what she was telling me probably was NOT her imagination, as she had suggested. I offered to loan her the book (even though I hadn't finished it) because I felt she needed to read it. She clutched it next to her heart, hugged me, and told me she would start reading it that night.

A few days later, Lynn returned the book with a "thank you" note and said that, as difficult as it was to read so soon after Gideon's death, it helped her! She still has one cat and, although she still mourns Gideon's passing, she drew comfort from knowing that he was still around.

Rob's Response: Our pets can guide us from the other side, and it became clear to me that Gideon influenced his mom, Lynn, to come to Keith's house that evening and talk about his passing knowing (likely with the help of a human spirit) that she would find comfort there. The physical feelings of Gideon's presence and the meow are typical signs that cats give us from spirit.

From Keith - "Of Skunks and a Coyote"
Rob - I also wanted to write about my friend, Steve. He's an old college roommate of mine who has struggled with his beliefs about the afterlife for as long as I've known him. I think that, after decades of thinking about the subject, Steve believes in some sort of

continuation of life, but does not believe in Christianity or any other organized religion.

Steve's father, who was a minister and an absolutely GREAT guy, passed away last month and this has really made Steve put even more thought into all this "afterlife" stuff. :)

I wanted to share Steve's story with you to get your thoughts. I just got the following message from him this morning:
"While spreading my dad's ashes at his favorite campus spots this evening after dark, my mom and I saw some skunks on the grounds of his fraternity and a coyote running across the parking lot just north of JRP then down the hill toward Memorial Stadium. Please interpret these sightings."

I'm not sure what sort of "sign" a skunk and a coyote would mean, but you don't really see these animals on our campus very often. Though a mutual friend who lives near the campus told us that there HAVE been skunk sightings lately. - Steve
Any thoughts? Keith

Rob's Response: Spirits, both human and animal often use animals or insects to convey their presence. Some examples previously cited include butterflies and dragonflies.

There may be no specific significance to seeing a skunk and coyote in this case, however. It's likely that those animals were the closest in the area for the spirit to use in order to show that he was present when his ashes were being distributed.

##

Chapter 30
Jacob's Buggy Sign and Musical Signs

The following email came to me and has been reprinted with permission, to help other grieving pet owners understand how their dogs (and cats) can communicate from the other side.

In this story, you'll learn how when it comes to spirit there is no such thing as a coincidence. In this case, an Amish buggy helped identify the spirit of this amazing dog.

From Bill - January 29, 2015:
Dear Rob - I am not sure where I stand in terms of believing what you wrote. Normally I would be very skeptical. In any event, I wanted to share our current situation.

Last week, 1/22/2015, we lost our Jacob. Jacob was a Sheltie and he died about 2 months before his seventh birthday. Jacob had lymphoma and despite every effort including chemo he lost his fight.

Jacob was my "baby." While I always liked dogs, they were pets. Jacob was the first animal that I completely gave my heart to. He came at a time in my life when I did not have much to live for. He gave my life meaning.

Jacob was born on an Amish farm in Lancaster County, Pennsylvania. He did not care much for horses and buggies and he would bark like mad whenever we passed one on the street. It was a game my wife and I would play with him pointing out all the buggies.

(Caption: Sir Jacob of Penn's Wood March 11, 2008 - January 22, 2015. Credit: Bill)

When Jacob passed I stopped eating and drinking. I went for three days with nothing to eat or drink. The average human can survive three to five days without drinking. This was going to be my exit.

Near the close of the third day my wife and I were sitting at a convenience store near our home getting gas. I have to say we live some distance from Lancaster and do not see horses and buggies where we live. After talking I decided to drink something. We had a bottle of water in the car that was for Jacob when we went somewhere. I drank some of the water ending my attempt at a passive suicide. At that moment a truck pulling a trailer passed in front of us. On this trailer was an Amish buggy. As I said, we just don't see buggies where we live. My wife and I broke down at first but then we considered the possibility that it was a message from Jacob. (All this happened before getting your book.)

Last night my wife was in a doctor's office waiting reading your book. A song came on "I Can't Live Without You." My wife, having just read where you talk about music, said "OK Jacob if that's you and if you're OK and someone is there taking care of you please send me a sign." The song ended and was followed by the song "The Wind Beneath My Wings." This is perhaps my wife's favorite song and holds very special significance for her since her father passed many years ago as it was his favorite song. The interpretation of this could mean that Jacob is OK and her dad is there with him.

Again, I don't know if I believe or not, but I have to say that I would like to. Believing would make live just a little more bearable. Bill

From Rob:

Those were amazing signs from him. Spirits lead us to places where we will see things that we'll associate with them, just as he enabled you to see the buggy (that drove him crazy). Perfect sign.

The musical signs are also great messages. The first song was directed to you, and the second song was the answer to your wife's request to prove the messages were from him. He's very strong, and will be around you from time to time. He doesn't want you to grieve, but instead wants you to know how much he appreciated you both saving him from a life of hardship on the Amish farm. He knows how much you did for him to try and heal him, and for that he is eternally grateful. You gave him more love in a day than he experienced in his life before you adopted him. That love binds you all together forever. I know the feeling with our two dogs who have passed and provide us signs from time to time.

With deepest sympathy, Rob

After receiving Bill's story, I asked if I could share it on my blog and in this book. He agreed. So, I decided to post Jacob's story on my blog a couple of weeks later - on Valentine's Day.

I later learned that it was Jacob who influenced me to post it on that particular day, so he could send another message to his pet parents!

From Bill:
Rob, Thank you for sharing this. Today was especially difficult for us because Jacob was always a big part of Valentine's Day for us. He always "bought" mommy a card and a present. ☺

I told Bill that I didn't know that about Valentine's Day being a special day, which explains why he insisted I post his story on that day. That was his "valentine" to his pet parents. Even pets acknowledge birthdays, anniversaries and holidays.

##

Chapter 31
A Picture Perfect Pup

In May, 2014 I collaborated with the Dachshund website "petmyweiner.com" to promote my first Pets book and have a giveaway. Some people submitted stories of how their pets communicated with them from the afterlife. Following is a story that the website picked to win a copy of the book, and the story is reprinted by permission.

In this story, you'll read about a special Dachshund named Oscar Mayer who influenced a friend of the pet parent to Photoshop his image in a painting that was meaningful to his mom and provided comfort.

Christine wrote:

Oscar Mayer was a special gift from Heaven for he was born on what would have been my parents 50 wedding anniversary. The first dog I would raise on my own from a puppy.

Oscar won the hearts of everyone including a local photographer. I was asked if he could photograph Oscar for a local T-shirt store to use for a sales promotion. I agreed.

Fast forward one year. Oscar developed a neurological disorder. He spent a week at the vets to no avail, it was evident when no medicine could pull him out of hours of seizures, and he would have to be put down.

As the vet prepared the lethal injection, I held Oscar tightly, from my mind to his, I asked him to give me a sign that he made it home to Jesus.

Three days later, I was closing the restaurant where I was employed, when a photographer named John Howard came knocking at the door. As I opened the door he asked me if I would like one more picture of Oscar. Tears filled my eyes as I said, "yes."

As I looked at the picture it was clear Oscar fulfilled my request. It's the picture of Jesus sitting on a rock with a child on his lap and others surrounding him. And at the feet of Jesus, laying on his favorite blanket was Oscar! My friend photo-shopped Oscar into the picture!

Absolutely no one knew of the request I made to Oscar, no one!

I wrote to Christine and informed her that she won the contest for my book. On June 7, she wrote me back with yet another sign from Oscar!

Christine wrote: I thought you would find this interesting... after replying to you email, I went over to Oscar's picture, (the one I sent you) and said, "We did it Oscar! We won! What do you think of that?"

Then I logged onto Facebook, yet again, I think he answered my question... the first post I seen... someone posted, "The Rainbow Bridge!" Irony or coincidence? I was unprepared for his answer! I think he approved!

Rob's Response:

Seeing the "rainbow bridge" posting at the time you asked a question is a direct response from Oscar. You're good at seeing the signs and that should be a great comfort.

Pets in spirit can hear us, because they are energy - and sound is energy. Every night I say goodnight to my dogs Buzz and Sprite, both of whom have passed and both have given me many signs they visit from time to time.

(Oscar Mayer Photo-shopped in a painting. Credit: John Howard, Photographer)

Oscar spends most of his time with your loved ones who crossed over and just visits you from time to time.

##

Chapter 32
Spirit Dog Sends a Real "Rainbow Bridge"

Our pets can get us to notice things in nature to let us know they're around. In this instance one special dog let her mom, Jan, know she was still around with her own "rainbow bridge."

I met Jan when I attended the New England Pet Expo in Wilmington, Massachusetts in 2014. I was joined by my friend Ruthie Larkin, also known as the Beantown Medium. Jan told Ruthie and me that she had lost her beloved Bassett Hound named Sissy.

However, she said that she recognized a sign from her after her passing. She asked his spirit to tell her if he had crossed the "Rainbow Bridge." The Rainbow Bridge is a popular poem about how animals cross into the light in the afterlife.
Jan was kind enough to share her story for everyone.

From Jan
Feb 17, 2000 will be a day I will never forget. On that Thursday I had to say goodbye to my best friend and confidant of 8 years and 3 months. Her name was Sissy and she was by far the most loving, sweet, loyal, affectionate, passive, perfect Basset Hound and she was my soul-mate dog.

Before taking her to the vets for the last time, I brought her to a Native American elder to bless her. He told me she was not dying but was just going to a different place and for me to watch for signs from her.

Almost immediately I started reading everything I could get my hands on about pet loss and quickly learned about the Rainbow Bridge.

I also found a wonderful website where I created a virtual cemetery space for Sissy, since I had her ashes sent to Arizona where I own a plot in a pet cemetery.

Well three weeks later to the date, March 9, I received 2 pieces of info in regard to Sissy. One was from the cemetery in Arizona saying they received her ashes and; they would be buried the next day. The other was from the website where I was creating the virtual cemetery and; they messaged me telling me that they had approved my submission and it would now be on line to view.

On my way home from work, on that very same date, I donated her leftover dog food to a stray dog rescue organization. As I was driving home it was raining, but the temperature was warm and nice. Still being dazed and confused throughout my intense grief, I thought to myself that Sissy gave me this weather. Then I spoke out loud "Maybe you can give me a rainbow, too."

Well, not more than a half mile later I saw people on both sides of the road, looking up at the sky. So naturally I also looked to the sky and there it was, the biggest, brightest rainbow I've ever seen in Massachusetts. It was so complete from end to end, beautiful and even with another smaller one behind it. Well I instantly started sobbing hard because all I could think of was my Sissy telling me something like, "I see it Mom. I see the rainbow and; I'm almost home." It was at that point, despite a ton of tears, I repeatedly thanked her for such an obvious, miraculous sign.

So, equally, March 9, 2000 will be a day I will also never forget.

(Photo: Sissy. Credit: Jan)

##

Chapter 33
Cody's Coins and Colors

In December of 2013, I received the following email about a Yorkie in spirit who kept influencing his mom to paint a room a certain color (and there's a reason why), and left a special coin to prove he is still around.

The movement of small objects from one place to another is called an "apport." Whether coins, feathers, or other small things, an apport is a common thing that spirits do to convey their presence.

From Cathy - Dec. 31, 2014:
Hi, my Yorkie Cody passed on the 23rd of this month. Of course I'm traumatized and I've been in tears every day. I had a feeling he was telling me to go on with my life and he wanted me to paint my bedroom gray, which I did a few days ago.

What was strange was I found a nickel with his date of birth while I was cleaning and painting under the armoire that was next to his bed. Also I had cleaned under the armoire a few days prior because I was compulsively cleaning to deal with his death. Anyways, I only looked at the date of the coin because I had read in your book that coins can be messages from spirits. Thanks.

From Rob Gutro:
Hi Cathy- Thank you for sharing that story with me. Spirits do influence us to think of things- and your thought to paint the room gray was likely influenced by Cody. Since dogs see many colors like red and brown in shades of gray, that would make sense.

(Photo: Cody. Credit: Cathy)

In addition, finding the coin with the date that matched his birth year was indeed a confirmation that he wanted to let you know he comes around from time to time, and is safely on the other side!

What a powerful connection you have with him. - Just know that he'll be there from time to time, but he finally got his message through that he's okay, so please take comfort in that.
Sincerely, Rob Gutro

From Cathy:
Hi, Rob, I didn't realize that dogs saw colors in shades of gray. I felt like painting my room gray before Cody passed on the 23rd when I knew in my heart he was going to pass soon.

Also, I thought it odd that I wanted to paint our bedroom gray because I love bright colors. Most of our house on the inside is purple. The kitchen is deep red, and I had our extra bedroom painted so yellow it's like the sun is always shinning in there. The picture I'm sending you is on the day I had Cody euthanized. I know you understand the pain of losing your baby. Thank you for getting back to me.

From Cathy:

Here's a picture of Cody's nickel.
I really have no idea how it got under the armoire or how I missed it when I cleaned under there when I cleaned the first time after his death and before I painted our room.

There was nothing else under there except dust balls.

(Photo: The nickel that Cathy found under the armoire. Credit: Cathy)

From Cathy:

The compulsion to paint my bedroom gray was so strong too after his death. I kept begging my husband until he relented. We painted it only six days after Cody passed.

From Rob:

Thanks for allowing me to share Cody's story with others. It will bring others hope and encouragement to look for signs from their dogs and cats. Wishing you and your family a happy new year (especially knowing that Cody is still around).

****

Dogs and cats are not entirely color blind. In fact, they can see yellow and blue. Those are the two main colors a dog can see. All of the other colors appear to them as shades of gray, so Cody gave Cathy his color of choice!

###

Chapter 34
Baldrick's and Mrs. Miggins' Signs

This chapter was written by Vittoria of New York, who is a cat mom who shared a special bond with two precious feline children. Vittoria experienced the passing of one of her cats and understood why he passed when he did, and then recognized signs he provided.

From Vittoria: A Rainbow from my Buddha-Boy

I adopted Baldrick and Mrs. Miggins (two cats) in 1997 from an attorney I worked for in New York City. After they were weaned, I went over to the attorney's apartment and decided that whichever two of this litter of four walked toward me would be the ones who chose me.

Baldrick was an orange striped tabby and Mrs. Miggins was a calico, and when I crouched on the floor in front of the litter, both of these little balls of fur came right to me. They grew to be very big, healthy, sweet kitties.

Mrs. Miggins had always seemed a little aloof, but Baldrick was so affectionate, even to the "strangers" (fellow Buddhists) who came to my apartment to chant, that he would walk right up to each and every person, look up into their faces, meow and rub his face on their leg or hand.

Baldrick and Chanting

Baldrick responded with total bliss at the sound of chanting. When my guests began doing Gongyo (reciting parts of the Lotus Sutra and chanting), Baldrick would go up to the front of the room, lie down in front of the altar and roll around in ecstasy on the floor. Even when I chanted on my own, he'd hear me ringing the bell to start Gongyo, come in from where ever he was, and lie down on my feet. When I was done, I would stand up and Balders would just gaze at me...but not right into my eyes. Rather, he would stare at the periphery around my shoulders and head. Apparently, my aura was exceptionally pretty after Gongyo.

(Photo: Mrs. Miggins and Baldrick. Credit: Vittoria)

Balders was also very empathetic. Over the 17 years he lived with me, I had some painful times, as we all do in life. I would sometimes sit on the side of my bed and cry. He would come in, gaze at me from the floor, then jump up on the bed, throw his 17-1/2 pound body against my lap and purr. That was his kitty hug. I'd pet him, but when I stopped, he'd immediate reach over and grab my hand back so I'd continue.

Baldrick had the loudest purr I'd ever heard. I'd be talking on the phone to my mother, who lived in Wisconsin, and hold the phone up to Baldrick, who loved lying on my chest while I was on the phone. I'd put the phone back to my ear and hear my mother laughing. "He sounds like an old Ford tractor," she said. (She died in August '13. She had never seen Baldrick; more about this later.)

(Photo: Baldrick waiting for me to come and chant; he's already blissed out. Credit: Vittoria)

Baldrick's Decline

Baldrick started losing weight during the summer of 2014. I knew his time was coming after a long life, and I also knew there was no way I could emotionally prepare for it. Over his lifetime, he'd wooed me and captured my heart, and I couldn't bear the thought of letting him go. During the month leading up to his transition, he seemed only partially connected with what was going on around him. Most of the time, he'd stare into the middle distance. He seemed so "out of it." How literal that phrase is: He was pulling "out of" this physical existence, and was more and more in non-physical.

On Thanksgiving, 2014 I was alone at home with the kitties. I had no dinner with anyone as I have no family in New York and both my sons live in other states, and was actually preparing to fly from New York to Kentucky two days later to spend my youngest son's birthday with him.

Although I had been making homemade food for Baldrick, he hadn't eaten much for the two days prior. When I brought my own lunch into the living room, where he'd been sleeping on the loveseat behind me, I heard a long, loud "MEOWWW!" and turned to see him looking at me. I was so relieved; he smelled my food and wanted some. I picked up the little bag of cheese I'd cut into tiny squares and, holding each piece to his mouth, he ate -- though it did seem like hard work for him.

About an hour later, having turned back to the computer, I heard a thump in the coffee table behind me. The coffee table was pushed up against the love seat where he was sleeping and apparently he had tried to get up. One of his forelegs had fallen into the crack between the table and the love seat, and in the process, he bumped his chin on the coffee table. He was not able to get himself out of that position. In that instant, I knew he was leaving.

Thinking that maybe he was trying to get up to go into the kitchen to have some food, I picked him up and carried him to his bowl. He walked away from it...or, rather, he walked with his forelegs, but his back legs dragged across the floor. I burst into sobs. I took him to the bedroom so that I could lie on the bed with him. That's when I noticed the drool on his chin. He laid on my chest for only a few seconds, then wanted down on the bed.

Remembering how much he loves chanting, I got up, put the chair in front of the altar, lit the candles and went in to get him. I laid him in my lap and started chanting softly. He struggled weakly; he wanted down. But as soon as I put him on the floor, he got into an old kitty playhouse the kitties got when they were small. I knew he *wanted to hide there to die. I got him back out. He then laid down on the floor in front of the altar. I chanted through sobs.*

I called my closest Buddhist friend, Fumiko, and told her Baldrick was dying. Fumiko loves my cats, and got such a kick out of the way Baldrick responded to chanting, both when she came over with a group and when she came alone to chant with me. She had just finished her Thanksgiving dinner and washed the dishes (it was, by then, about 7:30 at night).

Just as I ended that call, I turned to see Baldrick trying to drag himself toward my front door, as though he understood Fumiko would be coming over. I have a pair of drapes in the doorway between my foyer and my living room, and he came to rest with the drape directly over his back. He was, literally, half in the room and half out. He had NEVER done that before.

I picked him up and laid him back on the love seat and petted his bony body. I told him I loved him, and to purr for Nana (my mother) in heaven because she'd recognize him immediately.

Going to the Vet
After about half an hour, Fumiko called from the front door of my apartment building. I carried Balders in my arms down the eight flights of steps; no cat carrier needed this time. In the past, when I'd have to take him out of my apartment to go to the vet, he'd caterwaul very loudly in the hall. That night, he made no sound.

In the car, he would sporadically connect with what was going on and meow, struggling weakly. Fumiko and I would reassure him that we were there for him and loved him, and he would again relax in my arms.

Finally, we got to the 24-hour vet hospital in White Plains. Fumiko and I chanted softly as we walked to the front door. The lady there

163

knew who I was, as I'd called her, distraught, from home about 45 minutes earlier to make sure there was a vet on duty.

We were shown to a small room, where we laid Balders on an upholstered bench. He got up very weakly, and with great effort, turned in a half-circle, his head cast down. But then he collapsed again and before the vet came in, Fumiko and I resumed chanting softly. The vet entered with an assistant.

Saying Goodbye
Upon seeing Balders' bone-thin body, the vet said, "Yes, he's ready." Then he added, "Ordinarily, when I euthanize, I like to administer a sedative first, but he has no muscle left."

(I was thus spared the "what ifs" that, as I read in your book [Pets and the Afterlife], haunt so many humans; I knew beyond the shadow of a doubt that helping him to go was the right thing to do. Even more significantly, it became clear that Baldrick himself put this scenario together. More about that in a moment.)

They inserted the catheter in the inside of his leg as I held Baldrick's paws (he always loved "holding hands;" he'd tighten his "fingers" around my fingertip; this time, though, he had no strength). Fumiko was standing behind us; I was on my knees, gazing into Baldrick's eyes. We had explained to the vet that we are Buddhists and would be chanting. We did; Daimoku (the name for "Nam-myoho-renge-kyo," the phrase we chant) and a few "I love you's" were the last sounds Baldrick heard. I saw his eyes - not his pupils, but his eyelids - widen slightly and seem to focus. (I've had lots of death in my family recently and have been acquainting myself with many NDE accounts. I know how universal it is for people to see beyond the veil just before the moment of their transition. I will always wonder what Baldrick saw.)

Then his beautiful eyes went vacant. I looked over at his belly, and there was no more rise and fall. At that moment, the vet put his stethoscope to his heart. I asked if he was gone. The vet said, "Yes."

That first moment on the planet without my beloved Baldrick since he came into my life was excruciating. (Oh, boy, tears are falling as I type this...) I stood and put my arms around Fumiko, sobbing hysterically.

My Rainbow Request

Next day, I had to finish preparing for my trip to Louisville, Kentucky. Of course, I cried off and on all day. It was at LaGuardia airport that I began reading about animals and the afterlife.

On the flight, flying in the bright sunshine over clouds below, my attention was caught by a very, very bright spot of light below us. It appeared to have something to do with the sun on the mist, but it was bright white. With the stories of the ADC from pets still fresh in my mind, I said, softly, "Balders, give me a rainbow."

I kept my eye on that bright white light, and sure enough, once in a while it would appear to split into some soft color, but it was when I looked a few degrees to the left of it that, only about two minutes after I asked for it, that I saw a brilliantly colored "water dog."

Thank God I was sitting in a seat by myself, because I burst into tears again. "Thank you, Balders," I said.

"Thank you."

Incidentally, I think I finally found out what the bright spot was: Chembows, or sun shining through chemtrails. So even THEY were types of rainbows! And very mysteriously, the chembow stayed down and to the left of my plane for A FULL NINETY MINUTES.

165

Seriously, how does a chemtrail stay in the same position as we travel with it, unless a jet was flying under and just ahead of us? Maybe it was a reflection of glare coming off our plane and shining into the clouds below.

I do have photos and video, though I didn't have my camera out when the rainbow I asked Baldrick for appeared. (In fact, it never appeared again during the flight; only when I asked Baldrick for it.)

(Photo: The chembow as it began to split into color. Credit: Vittoria)

Given the two kinds of rainbow, it seems Balders wanted to make sure he got through.

Baldrick Waited to Pass

Another thing that Baldrick did, was time his passing so that he'd be surrounded by chanting, at a time when I could be with him. I work second shift, and since the beginning of his decline, was haunted by the fear of coming home from work and finding his lifeless body. This fear was heightened the past couple of weeks when I thought about going to Louisville for four days, leaving the feeding of the cats to two neighbors.

But think about it: He started the dying process while I was at home to witness it; I called Fumiko just as she finished her washing up after Thanksgiving. Baldrick was surrounded by love and chanting at the end; and I had another day off work to grieve before heading off to Kentucky. As painful as his transition was, it came during that *perfect, tiny window of time. This was his final gift to me: He and I needed to be together, with Fumiko present to hold me up in those first horrendous minutes of bereavement.*

As it turned out, Baldrick sent another sign five weeks later, when he returned in a dream with a message that puzzled me the morning after I had it, but became heartbreakingly clear the following day.

Mrs. Miggins Experiences Difficulty

On December 30, 2014, I was in the kitchen preparing food for Mrs. Miggins. She would always come to the kitchen if she heard me rustling around in there to ask for food or an ice cube for her water. But this day she wasn't, and I got a little spooked.

I found her in my bedroom, lying on my floor in front of my guitars, a part of the floor where I'd never seen her recline. She was lying on her side, staring straight ahead at, seemingly, nothing.

Next day, symptoms began to appear. She was grunting. Her breathing was labored. She'd be walking across the floor and suddenly begin to growl, as though she was in pain. She'd been perfectly healthy up until then – every day of her entire 17 year (that's 84 people years) life, in fact. Then, suddenly, she started exhibiting very scary symptoms.

Baldrick's Visit in a Dream

The following day was New Year's Day, and I woke up very late from an extremely vivid dream that felt more like a message. Because I've had dreams from The Other Side several times over the past couple of years due to deaths in my immediate family, I was beginning to learn how to discern those from dreams from ordinary ones.

In the dream, Baldrick appeared, but suddenly I was watching him in black and white. Next thing I knew, color came back and he was not alone, but had several other cats with him. That dream cast a long shadow over my whole day and added to my anxiety over Mrs. Miggins.

Mrs. Miggins Goes to the Vet

Next morning, I took her to the vet. She was taken to another room for an assessment; in a few minutes, the vet returned with the news: "She's extremely ill. She's already shutting down." I knew what had to be done. The vet said, "I'll go give her a sedative, then bring her to you so that you can be with her to the end."

Several minutes later, the vet appeared in the doorway -- without Mrs. Miggins -- and said, "I'm so sorry. She's already passed away." (I had no idea she was that close; later, I imagined her leaping out of her beautiful little body to be with her brother.)

A Paw Print

The vet asked if I wanted cremation; I did. But I didn't want the ashes. I explained that it was Mrs. Miggins' life force that was now gone. She wasn't in her body. The vet, and later the vet's assistant, asked if I wanted her Paw print. I didn't; after all, it would be an impression made by part of her lifeless body, and I couldn't take that.

On my walk back home, I reflected on the dream of the day before, and suddenly I understood. The black and white meant "fading life force." And it's pretty clear what it meant to see Baldrick with other kitties. He met his beautiful sister on Rainbow Bridge and brought her home. I also remembered how Mrs. Miggins was in my room on the floor, still relatively healthy just three days before, staring at "nothing." Just as people often get reassuring visits from their departed loved ones just before their own transitions, I now believe Mrs. Miggins, at that moment, received such a visit from Baldrick.

Still walking home from the animal hospital, crying, I thought of the rainbow that Baldrick gave me only two minutes after I asked for one, while I was on the plane to Louisville. I said, quietly through tears, "I don't suppose I could get a sign from you, too, could I, sweetie?" Immediately, I looked down at the sidewalk and [I saw one impressed upon the sidewalk].

(Photo: The paw print. Credit: Vittoria)

I couldn't bear a paw print from her physical body because she was no longer inside it, so she offered one from Non-Physical.

Goodbye, sweet Balders and Mrs. Miggins. Please meet me when it's my turn. I love you forever and ever. - Mama

##

Chapter 35
Getting Guidance from Our Pet's Spirits

Humans and pets can be influenced by spirits. Spirits of dogs, cats or people can suggest we do things, teach other pets to do something they did, or guide us to do something that we may not think about until we find ourselves doing it.

For example, we may turn away from a street we would normally take to drive home only to learn later that an accident happened on that street at the time we would have been traveling on it.

Dogs and cats who pass sometimes come back and "teach" our new pets right and wrong and help correct their behaviors. In fact, I've spoken with quite a number of people who lost pets and told me that their new pets demonstrate some of the same habits as their pet who passed. Of course, that would be easy to explain if their older pet was alive to teach the newer pet. But that's not the case.

So, people don't understand how their new pet could have the same habits as the pet who passed. The answer is that the new pet learned the habits from the spirit pet!

In Pets (book 1) I explained how the spirit of a Chihuahua named Chico told me he was around a large black dog, and was "teaching him the ropes." That was the first time I received that message and I've learned that it's very common.

The following experiences were shared with me via email that convey the same experiences. The first experience shows how one dog learned from another in the physical plane. This sets a good example of how it works between spirit and living dog.

The second account is about a cat's spirit influencing the behavior of the newly adopted cats.

What's important to keep in mind is that our pets behave *exactly* the same in spirit as they did in life.

Dog Influencing Behavior of Living Dogs

Donna said: *I lost 2 precious dogs the same day about one year ago on April 8th. They both fell ill within a week of each other and both spent the same weekend at the vet hospital.*

Hank had bladder cancer and was 11 years old. Sparkie has lymphocytic leukemia and was almost 4 years old. When Sparkie came home as a 10 week old pup, Hank was like is guardian angel and father figure to Sparkie. They had such a close bond.

Sparkie was a very "high anxiety" dog and looked to Hank for security. So when they passed the same day together... even though it was extremely hard on us as our family was losing 2 family members... Sparkie had his guardian angel in life go with him to the "Rainbow Bridge."

I miss them both so much. It still hurts every day. I know our Ally misses them too. She and Hank were very close... she is a Border Collie. Now we have a 1 ½-year-old GSD, he has so many personality traits that our Hank and Sparkie had... we will never forget our boys... but I can't seem to get it out of my head that Hank and Sparkie have a connection with our Poobear.

Cat Influencing Other Cats

Terri said: *We lost our Sweetums on February 4, 2007. We adopted 2 kitties 6 months later. However, no one could ever take Sweetums place.*

What's interesting is that Cosmo, our male kitty, has many actions and traits that our baby girl had...so sometimes we refer to him as "Sweetums!"

Dog Spirit Training

On December 20, 2015 I had an interview on the Jeff Richards Paranormal radio show from Saskatchewan, Canada. During the interview, Jeff had a caller describe that their current pet was showing the same habits as his new dog. The caller thought his new dog was the reincarnated soul of his dog that passed. Actually, the dog was being trained by the spirit of the dog who passed. You can hear the interview here: https://youtu.be/rlCctz-sgOE.

##

Chapter 36
Spirits Using Environment to Convey Signs

Spirits can manipulate things in nature such as birds, butterflies, dragonflies, feathers and flowers. They can also move coins, wind chimes or holiday ornaments. It takes energy to make these things happen, though, and spirits draw on the positive emotional energy of the love we share with them to help do that, as well as other physical energies that may be nearby (like heat, light, water or electricity).

Keep in mind that just because you see a bird or a butterfly after someone passes, it wasn't necessarily sent from the spirit. It's always healthy to be skeptical. Otherwise it's like thinking that every old house is haunted (and they're not).

One way you can tell if it's a message from spirit is if the bird, butterfly, etc. behave oddly. For example, if they linger around people (which is pretty unusual) and not skitter off after a person moves - that's odd. If a bird shows up at the same time every day and stares through the window of your bedroom, that's odd behavior. That actually happened when the spirit of teenage boy told me he sent a bird outside of his dad's window every day for a week after the boy passed. The father confirmed it for me.

The following are similar experiences people have shared with me. These are grouped together to show the different ways that spirit pets have used things in the environment to communicate with the living.

"Lexi's Persistent Butterfly" and a Meaningful Puddle
This account shows how persistent a spirit can be in letting their pet parent know that they're still around. A special dog named Lexi manipulated a butterfly to boldly give message after message that

she's still around her pet parents and she did it over the course of days and weeks!

Carol said: Hi Rob - I just wanted to let you know how much you books are helping me with the loss of my precious Lexi. She was the best dog we ever had. She was a mix that we rescued from the human society up here over 14 years ago.

She loved everyone and every dog she ever met.

She came to me the night of her passing, a puddle of water appeared on the floor where she had been having accidents. It was in a path where my husband and I walked all evening and it did not appear till right before I went to bed.

She passed at 12:57 p.m. that afternoon and we saw the puddle late that night at 1:00 a.m. in the morning.

[**Editor's Note:** The puddle is an incredibly personal sign and she did that to ensure that her mom and dad would know it was from her, because they had become so used to it.]

The next evening, a black and yellow butterfly appeared on a butterfly bush right outside of the window I can always see. I knew that she sent the butterfly to let me know she's around.

Then two days after the butterfly appeared, my husband and I were sitting on the patio where she loved to be with us. Suddenly a butterfly appeared and almost hit me in the face! Even my husband said "Look out!"

[**Editor's Note:** Lexi was really trying to get Carol's attention and ensure she didn't miss this appearance].

(Photo: Lexi's butterfly. Credit: Carol W.)

Immediately after coming near my face, the butterfly flew past, turned around and did the same thing to my husband! I can say that for the first time in his life he is a believer [in how spirit gives messages].

The butterfly then flew over to the bush and remained there for about five minutes. Then the butterfly flew over to the lot next to our house and flew around for what seemed another 5 minutes.

We understood that the butterfly was being influenced by Lexi, because we used to take her over to the other lot and let her run (which she had not been able to do the last couple of years).

[**Editor's Note:** So Lexi was doing the same thing she liked to do in the physical world.]

The butterfly appeared again two days later on Monday, and circled around me. Once again the butterfly flew over to [Lexi's favorite] field before disappearing.

On Tuesday morning, the Butterfly [Which by that time I thought of as Lexi's spirit] again appeared when I took the rest of the girls [dogs] out for their morning duties.

(Photo: Lexi. Credit: Carol W.)

I didn't see her again until Friday. That morning I had called the vet and they said Lexi's ashes were ready for pick up. When I took the girls out before we left to collect Lexi's ashes, there was the butterfly sitting in the tree where she and my grandson played for many years together!

It gave me goosebumps. [**Editor's Note:** But Lexi wasn't done. She had at least one more appearance to acknowledge that her mom and dad safely had her ashes.]

After we left the vet's office with Lexi's ashes, on the way home a black butterfly flew right across the path of our car.

My husband and I just looked at each other and said "Lexi."

Editor's Note: I checked in with Carol many months later in December of 2015, and she provided me with this update:

Carol said: *Yes, she [Lexi's butterfly] appeared on our butterfly bushes frequently over the summer. She would always land so she could be seen out our back window. She would actually sit on the bush till we came out an acknowledged her. We would sit very still* *and she would fly from my husband to me then fly over to the field next to her house.*

Ringing Chimes

I received an email from a woman named Gina who told me that when she thought of her pets, her wind chimes would ring. The ringing chimes are a sign that her pets are with her and were acknowledging their presence. It takes energy to move things and the spirit of her pets were drawing in the energy of her love (a positive emotional energy) to ring the chimes.

Movement, Butterfly and Visible Appearance

Debi said: *Rob - Hello, my name is Debi, we met at Paracon in Pensacola, Florida. We talked about my dog Brandy.*

We had her for three very short years, got her when she was a pup. I'll just say she picked me. This is how it happened: when I was at a friend's house her neighbors puppy came and sat by me and wouldn't leave my side, she came home with me that day.

Brandy was three when she died. That day was one of the worst days of my life. Not long after she passed, I realized she never really left. When she was here, physically, she would come into my bedroom and sit next to my bed, more like flop, and the bed would jerk. Many mornings I have awoken to that familiar jerk.

One day at my neighbors, I opened the door to leave, a large monarch butterfly was there, that butterfly stayed about ten feet in front of me and led the way home, when I stepped on my porch, it flew away.

Seven months after Brandy died, my grandson stayed the night. The next morning I woke up and he asked if we got another dog. "No," I told him. He proceeded to tell me he saw a dog come down the hall, turn into the kitchen and was just gone. I know Brandy never left, she's just waiting for us to join her.

Special Holiday Sign with an Ornament

I received an email from my friend Katharine who lives across the country. In the email, she conveyed an amazing sign from her English Setter who had passed before Christmas.

As I've said throughout this book and my other books, when it comes to spirit there's no such thing as a coincidence. Spirits can influence things to happen.

(Photo: Murphy. Credit: Katharine S.J.)

Katharine said:

I just had to tell you a really neat story. I lost my English setter Murphy two days before Christmas this year and was feeling like the house is rather empty and wishing she could let me know how she is. Some friends were over yesterday evening and I heard an ornament fall off the tree.

I looked over there and an English setter ornament had fallen off the tree and I felt like Murphy was saying hi to me!

Katharine sent a follow up note: *It was such a special sign from my Murphy and I am so glad I didn't miss it! That same night, my friends and I continued on out to eat. One of the specials was à la orange which was my late husband's favorite dish, so of course I believe that was a sign that he was telling me that Murphy was with him and saying hi.*

Editor's Note: The timing of Katharine's late husband's favorite dinner with the dropping of the ornament was even more of a connection. It was a confirmation that Murphy is indeed with his dad.

Bailey's Ball, Bounce and Book

A story was emailed to me and showed three different ways that the spirit of a little dog was able to send a message of his presence around his family after he passed. He conveyed his presence through a ball, a bounce and a book.

Lori's dog Bailey, passed in 2009, and sent her signs on at least two occasions. The first sign occurred more than 6 months after Bailey passed.

Lori was feeling guilt about his passing, as pet parents do when they have to make the decision to pass with dignity during sickness. Lori asked for forgiveness and a sign that he was okay and that he forgives me. Bailey's first sign came soon afterward.

Lori said: *My parents called to meet them at my sister's house for dinner. I cleaned myself up, and headed over with my new pup in tow. When I got there, I pulled out some toys I had left there for when I brought my dogs to visit. After we ate dinner, my sister and I were sitting at the table chatting when my nephew Tyler, who was five at the time, approached me with one of the dog toys. He said, "This is Bailey's favorite toy. It's Bay's ball. He likes it when it*

181

squeaks." Then he squeaked it repeatedly before setting it on the table next to me and put his hand on my shoulder saying, "Aunties, Bailey loves you."

(Photo: Bailey. Credit: Lori G.)

The second time I received a message [that Bailey is still around] was on the three-year anniversary of his passing. My mom had to have surgery that day, and since the hospital was close to the campground they go to, they had stayed there the night before. I was getting ready for work (at around 4 a.m.). I was in the living room putting my shoes on. I said out loud to Bailey, "I love you and miss you so much, but I need you to do me a favor. Grandma's having surgery today and I'm worried about her. I need you to go watch over her and make sure she's okay."

I no sooner got the words out of my mouth when I heard the distinct sound of a dog jumping out of my bed. All three of my dogs turned their heads to look down the hall where my room is (I was the only one home).

The surgery went fine. Later in the evening, my sister called to see how I was doing, knowing it was going to be a rough day for me. I told her about my morning experience, and that the day wasn't too bad because I knew Bailey was hanging around. We hung up, but a bit later, she called me back. She had gone through my nephew, Tyler's, book bag, and found a book he had gotten from the library that day. The title, **"Bailey Goes Camping."** *I guess he wanted to make sure I knew he was listening.*

Editor's Note: Sound is energy, and that's what spirits are- so when Lori made the plea to Bailey to give her a sign he heard her.

It's not surprising that Bailey got through to Lori's five year-old nephew Tyler. Children have a good connection with spirits (and earth bound ghosts if there are any around). Their logical minds are not yet developed, so they believe what they see and hear (from the spirits) and don't dismiss anything as we do as adults. Kids are much more intuitive! So, when Tyler was squeaking the ball, Bailey's spirit was right there! Obviously, Tyler knew that Bailey liked it, and squeaked it for him! How awesome! It sounds like Tyler was playing with Bailey's spirit. I think that's the first time I've heard that - and that is so cool.

The second sign of a sound of a dog bouncing or jumping off Lori's bed after asking for Bailey's help to cope with her grandma's surgery is also a clear sign that he heard her. It was also an action that he did when he was in the physical world.

Dogs will do things in Spirit that they would do in the physical world to send signs. The fact that Lori's other dogs heard it is more than enough confirmation.

The third sign of the book with Bailey's name in the title is another amazing way that spirit works. Bailey was really influencing Lori's nephew to pick up and read that book. I've learned that when it comes to Spirit, there truly is no such thing as a coincidence!

Bailey's love is a binding force that keeps bringing him around.

I love receiving emails like Lori's and the others in this book that provide proof, hope and comfort our beloved dogs and cats are still around us from time to time.

###

Chapter 37
A Pet's Spirit Makes a Winner - Influences

This story was conveyed to me at the Richmond, Virginia Pet Expo. This amazing story was shared by two attendees who are friends and neighbors. Right after I gave my lecture about my book "Pets and the Afterlife," two women came over to speak with me.

Signs from a Neighbor's Spirit

One of the women, I'll call her Mary, had a tiny peach colored teacup poodle in her arms who she couldn't cuddle enough. Mary said that the dog belonged to her late neighbor Connie. Connie knew that her time on earth was coming to an end soon and told Mary that she just wants to make sure her poodle is safe in a good home. Mary said if none of Connie's children would adopt the dog, she would take the dog.

Connie made sure that Mary would adopt the dog. Before Connie passed, she placed a note-turned-last-will on her kitchen table before she went to the hospital for the first time, stating "My neighbor Mary is adopting my dog." So it was.

The Dog's Grief

Mary said that she knows the dog has been grieving and seems to be aware of Connie's passing. She said that the tiny dog's eyes had streaks of tears for two weeks, and the little dog can't cuddle closely enough to Mary. Yes, dogs grieve, just as they do when another pet dies. One thing I've learned from pet spirits (yes, to some it would sound crazy) is that they often want us to get another dog and give him/her the love that was given to them.

Neighbor's Spirit Influences a Win

The other woman (I'll call Betty) who was with Mary, didn't have a dog. But Betty noted that all of Connie's (the late neighbor) feral cats had come into her yard when Connie passed (and there was no food outside anymore) looking for food. Betty said she began to feed them. There were several feral cats. Just before she came to the Pet Expo, she was trying to figure out how she could afford cat food for many feral cats*! That's when Connie's spirit stepped in.*

Spirits have a way of influencing us to do things for our benefit. Betty and Mary both said they weren't planning to come to the Pet Expo, but decided last minute "as if being pushed" (said Mary). When they got there, Mary needed to hear how I talked about a spirit's influence on our decisions. So did Betty. As soon as they arrived, they heard about a Karaoke contest and entered it singing *"Cats in the Cradle."* So, I asked what happened. Betty said, "We won $1,000.00 worth of cat food, can you believe it?"

Yes, That's Exactly How Spirits Work
Connie's spirit had pushed Mary and Betty to the expo knowing that Mary needed to know about influencing spirits and the grief the little dog was showing was real. Betty needed to be able to afford to feed Connie's feral cats and now she can.

Bottom Line
Next time you think people (or pets) on the other side can't influence you for the better, they can.

##

Chapter 38
Weezer's Wave, Flowers and Photo

When it comes to spirit, there are no such things as coincidence (as I've mentioned throughout this book). Spirits can manipulate things in nature and influence us to turn on a computer, a radio or television at the exact time needed to see something to remind us of them. Those are some of the things that a special Havanese dog named Weezer did to comfort his grieving pet parents.

Following is a story that Weezer's mom shared about the signs that he provided after his passing.

Marie B. said: Hello Rob, we had the pleasure of meeting at the New England Pet Expo and I told you of my beloved dog Weezer and the wonderful signs we have received from him.

On Monday April 15th it was an unusually warm day. We dropped our Havanese named Weezer at the vet's office for a routine dental cleaning. When we picked him up in the late afternoon they told us they needed to extract 11 very large teeth and due to decay were unable to suture his gums.

We took him home and later that evening he was bleeding so badly we rushed him to a local emergency clinic. They were able to stabilize him over the night and pack his mouth but were unable to reach his vet to have the records transferred. The next day he needed to be rushed into Angell [Animal Medical Center] in Boston.

There he remained in intensive care for the next three days. His humans visited him as often as possible.

(Photo: Weezer the Havanese. Credit; Marie B.)

They were beyond wonderful at Angell and did their best but this little guy could not get his blood to clot, his vitals stable and the infection under control.

Our last visit was very late in the day on the 18th. He looked up from his crate and stared into my eyes. With all of his strength he raised his paw up and down as if to say good bye.

The next morning after talking to the ED Doctor we decided to go into Boston to see Weezer - but shortly after hanging up they called back and said he gave out a little yelp and passed peacefully. Weezer died on April 19, 2012 on his 10th birthday.

My heart broke – this dog could read into my soul like no other pet I have ever had. He saved me the agony of deciding to euthanize him but left me wondering if he suffered to die all alone. I ached to have had the chance to hold him in his final hours.

(Photo: The Dogwood Tree blossomed. Credit: Marie B.)

We went into Angell to say our goodbyes. We returned home later that day to find that our dogwood tree (where we have all of our pets ashes buried under) had blossomed beyond anything that we had *ever witnessed. I took this as a sign that he was at peace and was not upset that I was for not there at the time of his passing.*

A few weeks later I was still in mourning and missing him. We had received his ashes a few days before. I was getting dressed for work and talking to Weezer asking him to send me a sign he was okay. I looked in the mirror and saw that my outfit was identical to the way Weezer looked. All in black with a white "V" blaze from my neck to my belt. Thank you buddy!

Then on July 2 – which was 10 years to the date that we brought him home to live with us I opened the boston.com website and there was a caption "For all you dog lovers" along with a picture that looked identical to our Weezer.

I welcome all of these signs from him knowing that even with his passing nothing will break the bond between us.
Warm regards, Marie

##

Chapter 39
The Amazing Signs of a Cat Named Mr. D.

Jeff and Stacie had a cat named Mr. D., short for "Diablo." He was like a son to them, and when he passed, they were devastated. Mr. D. however, wanted to let them know that his time in the physical plane may have been over, but his time in the spiritual plane gave him opportunities to communicate that he didn't have before.

Who Was Mr. D.?
Mr. D was a feral cat who came with the house that Jeff and Stacie purchased. Jeff said that he laughed at the fact that the previous owners of the house named him "Diablo," which is Spanish for "Devil." He and Stacie thought it ironic that such an "absolute angel of a creature ended up with the name Diablo."

The previous homeowners described Diablo as a "mysterious huge black cat that came around from time to time in the night. They said they never had much interaction with him since he kept his distance, but looked menacing in the darkness with his large frame.

During the first week in their new home in 2002, one evening, Jeff and Stacie were greeted by Diablo while they were in the garage. They described their initial feelings as being a little nervous, given his size, but those feelings quickly disappeared as Diablo came over to them, rubbed against their legs, and when Stacie sat down, Diablo jumped in her lap. They realized he was homeless and not neutered. He left, but visited every night for weeks and began to sleep in their garage. They thought this black cat could not possibly be the cat the previous homeowner called "Diablo" because this cat demonstrated gentle behavior.

Although they had never taken a feral cat into their family before, Jeff said he felt a connection, took him to the vet to get his shots, neutering, etc. and welcomed Diablo into the family.

Jeff said, "Over the years, that cat taught me the true love that can be found between animal and human and completely changed my outlook on life and our relationship with God's living creatures. A seemingly simple cat, who could not speak with words, opened my eyes and taught me so many wonderful things that no human ever could. For that, and for so much else, he will never be forgotten."

(Photo: Mr. D. Credit: Stacie and Jeff B.)

Mr. D's Passing

In May of 2012, Mr. D. wasn't feeling well. He was sickly, lethargic, and his veterinarian told Jeff and Stacie that they need to embrace what little life Mr. D. had left. Mr. D was diagnosed with diabetes in 2006 and had several health scares that he had bounced back from. However, his veterinarian's grim prognosis this time was that Mr. D only had less than two weeks to live.

Despite the sad news, Jeff was determined that Mr. D would still be around to make it to their semi-annual trip to visit family in Michigan for the 4th of July. Mr. D really enjoyed traveling, especially to the

Michigan lake house where Jeff's mom lived. Somehow, Mr. D did beat the odds and was still doing as well as could be expected when it came time to drive from Maryland to Michigan in July of 2012.

Mr. D did enjoy his lake house vacation, however, when it came time to leave for home, Mr. D was uncharacteristically hiding under a bed. He was pulled out and looked sickly. They decided to make the drive home rather than find a vet in Michigan since Mr. D. had bounced back from a few of these episodes before.

The most difficult decision a pet parent can make is to decide when it's time to let their pets go to the afterlife. The act of bringing our loved ones to a vet is just heart-wrenching. Some vets will actually come to the house, so a pet can pass in familiar surroundings. Other times, people choose to have their pets pass peacefully at home (as long as the pet is not in pain). In this case, Mr. D. passed peacefully in Jeff's arms as Stacie continued to drive home.

Jeff said, "I had Mr. D. in my lap and was petting him around 10 p.m. As we drove through the mountains of Pennsylvania, he let out a couple of deep sighs and then left us." They feel that it was probably the best way for him to pass, peacefully with Jeff holding and petting him wrapped in his favorite blanket.

Because it was late, they took him home, and laid him at the foot of their bed, wrapped in his blanket, until he could be brought to the vet the next morning.

The Grief, Guilt, Denial
Many pet parents suffer grief and guilt after a pet passes, wondering if they did the right thing. Some wonder if they should've let their pets pass in their sleep even if in pain, while others agonize over euthanizing their pet. Others, like Jeff and Stacie, tried to deny that he had passed, but finally accepted it.

Overnight, Jeff got up and loosened the blankets around his face, just in case he had started breathing again. He said he went downstairs and came across a small box that contained Mr. D's insulin which they gave him twice a day for his diabetes over the last 6 years of his life. Jeff broke down at the sight of it. He said he put it in the refrigerator thinking "just in case he wakes up tonight."

When he returned to the bedroom, he checked on Mr. D's lifeless form again, "just to be sure." Jeff went to sleep and awoke the next morning hoping to see that Mr. D. came to and moved.

By 10 a.m. on Monday, twelve hours after Mr. D. passed in the car on the ride home, Jeff said that he finally acknowledged Mr. D's passing.

Mr. D. was cremated and his remains were placed in a nice box to honor his memory.

Jeff corresponded with a close friend after Mr. D's passing to help cope with the loss. His feelings were similar to many pet parents. He said in an email "I have lost parents, family members, close friends, acquaintances and childhood pets, but nothing has affected me so deeply as losing Diablo (Mr. D.)."

Getting Used to the Emptiness
Since Mr. D. passed in the car, the car became a reminder of his last moments. Jeff and Stacie have other cats, and when they heard something fall off the credenza where Mr. D. used to like sitting, they called out "Mr. D, stop knocking things off the credenza!" - and then realized it was one of their other cats.

Their friend Zimmie told Jeff and Stacie that they will probably hear noises in the night for a very long time, and it will be Mr. D walking around in spirit. Zimmie told them that she's grateful when she hears her cats in spirit walking around. That was good advice as

Mr. D. had plans to let Jeff and Stacie know he was still around them.

Signs from Mr. D.

On July 11, 2013, the same day that Stacie received the phone call that Mr. D's ashes were ready for them to pick up, Mr. D. made his first appearance in what was considered "his bathroom." It was there where Jeff and Stacie had administered his insulin shots over the previous six years, and all the diabetic supplies were stored. They said it was a room where they spent a lot of time caring for him, and it was not open to their other cats.

Jeff said "when I opened the door to enter the bathroom, before turning the light on, I was startled to see a dark black mass sitting on the floor shaped exactly like a cat!" He blinked and looked again and it still sat there on the floor. "I turned the light on expecting to see another one of our cats who had snuck in there," Jeff said. "There was nothing there. The floor was bare, but I knew that I had seen a cat's shape there and it wasn't an illusion."

Jeff wanted to recreate the shape, so he turned off the light, stepped out of the bathroom and re-entered and turned the light on. He said he did it several times until Stacie asked what he was doing. He realized that it was Mr. D, and silently thanked Mr. D for the visit.

Suddenly after that there was a second sign. Jeff said he was startled by a loud "clank" on the floor after thanking Mr. D. "I looked down to find a heavy steel can of hairspray had somehow 'fallen' from our bathroom counter to the floor and rolled over to the spot where I saw the cat on the floor." Jeff said that he knew Mr. D had to have knocked it over, because the can had been in the middle of the counter for weeks, nowhere near the counter's edge.

No sooner did Jeff walk into the living room to tell Stacie what had just happened, that his third sign became apparent. Jeff said "I got emotional, went into the living room and tried to explain to Stacie what I just witnessed. She, too, became very emotional and we stood and embraced in the middle of our living room. As we stood there holding each other, Stacie just happened to look up through our skylight and gasped 'Look!' Despite a blue sky and no rain in the forecast, there was a cloud with a beautiful rainbow stretched across it!" They went outside and took pictures of the rainbow that lasted about 10 minutes. Shortly after it faded, they noticed a cloud that appeared to be shaped as a cat angel.

The rainbow was especially meaningful, because after Mr. D. passed, Stacie had read the poem about the "Rainbow Bridge" over and over again. That poem is about a place that pets go after they pass.

They knew that it was Mr. D. sending all of those signs. They said that these signs brought them so much peace.

Depression in Other Pets
Cats and dogs experience depression just as people do. After Mr. D. passed, Jeff and Stacie noticed that their cat "Shady," a grandson of Mr. D's, was exhibiting depression. He yowled frequently as he went room to room as if he was looking for Mr. D, especially after Jeff and Stacie returned home from trips, since Mr. D usually accompanied them on trips.

Shady and Mr. D. were inseparable, and when Mr. D. passed, Shady became a "lap cat." It was odd behavior, because Shady never wanted to sit on anyone's lap. Further, when they went to bed, Shady followed them to the bedroom, jumped on the bed and slept with them. "It was new and welcome behavior from Mr. D's best friend," Jeff said.

Another Rainbow Bridge

Stacie said that when she picked up Mr. D's ashes and opened the folder holding his cremation certificate, inside was the "Rainbow Bridge" poem with a drawing of a rainbow.

Physical Signs from Mr. D.

On July 23, 2012, Mr. D. gave a physical sign and the timing was another confirmation.

Jeff came home from work and took a nap as Stacie took their dog out for a walk. He said there were no cats in their bedroom, and he closed the door, turned off the light and fell asleep. He was awakened by the sound of a heavy plastic bag full of stuff falling in the room. He felt something brush against is back while still lying down and trying to focus on the sound. Then a feeling of something brushing by the back of his neck and back of his head.

He turned on the light and noticed it was exactly at 10 p.m.

The bag was filled with towels and had been sitting firmly against their large dresser for about a week.

He got up, puzzled and went downstairs where he found Stacie. He asked if she let a cat in the bedroom or entered the room. She hadn't gone in the room, and there was no cat in the bedroom. But there was a cat in the room, in spirit and the timing was impeccable.

Stacie had Jeff go into the living room where she had lit three candles around a little "shrine" to Mr. D. that they made that contained his ashes, photos, lock of his fur, tracings of his paws and favorite toys. From 9 to 10 p.m. on Monday nights, Stacie connected to a pet loss website to honor pets that passed. Stacie said right before 10 p.m. she said a little prayer telling Mr. D. how much she missed him and that he can come anytime and visit.

There are no such things as coincidence when it comes to spirit. Stacie asked Mr. D. to visit around 10 p.m. and he made an appearance upstairs where he woke Jeff up by knocking over the bag of towels and brushing against him! What's also interesting is that Mr. D. passed around 10 p.m. and that's the same time he made a return appearance.

Maintaining the Personality and Habits

When people or pets pass their soul or energy couple with their memories and personalities. Mr. D's personality remained intact, according to Jeff and Stacie. "In life, Mr. D was always knocking things over as he maneuvered his big body around places he should not be." Just as he knocked over the can of hairspray in the bathroom during his first appearance and knocked over the heavy bag of towels on his second visit."

"We loved him so much that we usually just let him climb around on whatever it was he was climbing on and then picked up all the stuff he knocked over with a smile and a shake of our head," Jeff said. "In the afterlife, he seems to be keeping his old habits intact."

Mr. D's Frame Trick

On July 26, 2012, Mr. D appeared to do the impossible with a frame that held his photo.

Stacie found a silver picture frame from their "Mr. D. shrine" on the floor when she came home. She said that it's a silver cat-shaped frame with a little silver metal fish that was hanging from the cat's mouth. "There is a solid metal ring on the fish's mouth that attaches to a metal ring on the cat's mouth, to give it a dangling effect," Stacie said. She noticed the fish was laying separately from the frame and a couple of feet away from it when she found it.

*(Photo: Mr. D's trick separating the fish from the frame.
Credit: Stacie and Jeff B.)*

When Jeff came home she asked him to try and re-attach the fish to the frame. He couldn't. The ring was solid with no break. The ring on the cat's mouth had "the thinnest imaginable gap, about 5 times thinner than the ring on the fish," Jeff said. There was no possible physical way for that fish to have come off that ring.

"We were just left with the reality again of having no explanation other than Mr. D having something to do with it," Jeff said. "He is definitely showing his communication method of choice through making things fall (or knocking them over)." They left the fish detached as a reminder of how amazing things can be sometimes, especially when it comes to spirit.

Three Years Later

On July 8, 2015, Stacie wrote to Rob: *Hi Rob! Today is the 3 year anniversary of our beloved dearly departed "Mr. D's passing. Jeff and I have been thinking a lot about him lately. Would you believe that while spot cleaning a blanket that was very similar to Mr. D's favorite blanket the other day outside on my deck a butterfly landed on the blanket I was cleaning... sat there for a minute, then flew and landed on my leg for a minute or two, then flew to the nearby deck railing and sat there a while as I was working. I don't think I have ever had a butterfly land on me before! Well, of course I know you would believe it.*

Editor's Note: Because spirits have the ability to influence things in nature, like butterflies, birds, feathers, etc. it's easy for them to send us a sign that way.

Thank you for informing me of signs to look for... I know that was Mr. D's doing again. Absolutely amazing. I feel so blessed to have had him in my life and STILL have him in my life.

Later that night of the anniversary, Stacie was outside on the deck with her dog. He started barking at something in the dark, so Stacie peeked around the corner of the house and saw the shadow of a cat sitting at the corner of the front of the house. The cat sat there for a minute and then took off running into the woods. It very well may have been Mr. D dropping by.

THE END... (For now)

###

Conclusion

Energy cannot be destroyed, but it can be changed. After physical lives end, the energy within humans and animals combines with memories, personalities and knowledge of this lifetime and becomes chooses to stay earthbound as a ghost or crosses into the light and becomes a spirit.

Almost all of our pets cross over into the light because our loved ones in spirit are there to greet our pets and welcome them over.

The spirits of our loved ones also let us know they are around us. They will come to us whenever we call to them, see a photograph of them or think about them. Spirits come into our dreams to let us know they are fine (ghosts don't seem to have that capability to enter dreams). Spirits of our pets will be waiting for us when it is our time to pass to welcome us into the next life.

It is my experience that love never truly dies, and it even transcends from the afterlife to this life. Just keep an open mind, watch for signs and understand that life continues after the physical body is gone.

Mediumship is a Puzzle You Have to Put Together

Sometimes the person to whom a message is intended won't immediately understand the significance of a message. Other times, it may be as clear as a butterfly landing near you.

You may also receive messages for the friend of a friend. That's because although that person may not be receptive, they know you may be, and will share the message with the person for whom the message is intended. Spirits work hard to let us know they are around.

Don't be discouraged if you don't understand something – you may figure it out in time.

Sometimes it's difficult to understand the messages from spirit, and it's easy to mistake their identity. For example, if you find pennies and think it's your late cat, it could very well be a message from your grandmother, or vice versa. You need to study the clues, check what date it is, including the date on the coin. Those things could hold clues to the spirit's identity.

During one of medium Barb Mallon's events, I physically saw the spirit of a well-dressed older African-American gentleman sitting next to a woman in the audience. The man's spirit told me that he was connected to the young woman.

I assumed (and I shouldn't have) that because the male spirit looked older than the young woman in the audience, that he was a father or grandfather, so I told her that. She was puzzled. I told her the man's spirit watching over her is a "sharp dresser" and loved wearing hats. He was also very dedicated to his Bible and his faith.

At the time, she told me both her grandfathers died when she was young. She was sure that the spirit was not either of them. She left disappointed and confused, and I was puzzled. The spirit was so adamant that he was connected to her.

One week later, the young woman emailed Barb Mallon and said that after discussing my reading with her father she realized the spirit was that of her uncle!

She said that her dad broke down into tears when she told him all the signs I provided. She said her father's brother passed away and my messages made perfect sense to her dad. She told Barb to thank me for providing her dad comfort and assurance that his brother was still around and looking after his niece. The lesson I learned from this is not to assume that a spirit is a certain relative, but either an elder or a contemporary (meaning the same age), or someone younger.

Messages from Spirit are a puzzle we all have to piece together to get the answers and you don't have to be a medium to get them! You can get messages, too. Just before going to bed each night ask your loved ones to come into your dreams and keep pen and paper on your nightstand so you can record them when you wake up.

A Final Note: Honoring Your Pet
If you want to honor the memory of your beloved pet, the best thing you can do is to adopt another who is in desperate need of a home. Contact a rescue and save a helpless animal, and share the love you have for the pet you may have lost with another. Our pets that pass tell me that the best way to honor their memory is to help another.

If you're not ready to adopt another pet, volunteer at a shelter or donate to a rescue.

If your friends want to provide comfort to you during your time of grief, ask them to make a donation to an animal rescue in your pet's name. That's a wonderful way to memorialize your pet, and another way to make your pet's spirit smile from the other side.

To read more about ghosts and spirits, pets or people, visit my blog at: *www.robgutro.com* or *www.petspirits.com*

With Appreciation

This book would not have been possible without the assistance, time and personal stories from a number of people and /or their special companions.

My thanks to my husband for editing and improving the book, and spending many nights with our dogs watching television while I worked on the book and made arrangements for appearances, interviews, and answered emails. I am honored to include the personal stories from so many wonderful people that I've met as a result of my first volume of "Pets and the Afterlife."

I hope that by sharing their stories, this book has given them comfort to know that their beloved family member will be immortalized in print, and that their stories have given others comfort and understanding that their pets are also waiting for them and around them from time to time.

###

Bibliography

Chapter 3: Pets Are More Intelligent Than We Think

Burns, Gregory; How Dogs Love Us: A Neuroscientist and His Adopted Dog Decode the Canine Brain; 2013; New Harvest Inc., New York, N.Y.

Coren, Stanley; The Intelligence of Dogs; 2006, Pocket Books, Simon & Schuster, UK.

Coren, Stanley; How Dogs Think, 2004, Free Press a division of Simon and Schuster, New York, N.Y.

Grandin, Temple; Animals in Translation; 2006; Harcourt, Orlando, Fla.

Hare, Brian and Woods, Vanessa; The Genius of Dogs; 2013, Dutton, New York, N.Y.

Hare, Brian and Woods, Vanessa; Dognition.com website

###

About the Author

Rob is an avid dog lover who, with his partner, volunteers with Dachshund and Weimaraner dog rescues. Together, they've fostered and transported many dogs, assessing the dogs at shelters for the rescues, working with coordinators, vets, and shelters to save the lives of dogs. They have four dogs, a Weimaraner, two Dachshunds and a Dachshund-Chihuahua mix.

(Photo: Rob with Dolly, Franklin and Tyler. Credit: Tom W.)

Rob considers himself an average guy, who just happens to be able to hear, feel, sense and communicate with Earth-bound ghosts and spirits who have passed on.

When not communicating with the dead, Rob communicates with the living. He's a meteorologist by trade who enjoys talking about weather. He speaks at schools, museums, and social organizations about weather. Rob worked as a radio broadcast meteorologist at the Weather Channel. He has almost 20 years of on-air radio broadcasting experience.

Rob enjoys taking ghost walks in various cities and visiting historic houses and sites to see who is still lingering behind and encourages them to move into the light to find peace.

He still reads and collects comic books and has always loved the mysterious heroes. Since he was a boy, one of his favorite superheroes has always been the ghostly avenger created in the 1940s called "The Spectre."

Rob does provide limited pet spirit readings and details are on his website. If you would be interested in having Rob give a lecture, appearance or rescue fundraiser, please contact him through email or his blog.

To share stories or questions write Rob at Rgutro@gmail.com
Amazon Author Page: https://tinyurl.com/vzy7kre
Blog: www.robgutro.com or www.petspirits.com
http://ghostsandspiritsinsights.blogspot.com/
Facebook pages: www.facebook.com/RobGutroAuthorMedium
www.facebook.com/ghostsandspirits.insightsfromamedium
Twitter: https://twitter.com/RobGutroAuthor
YouTube: https://tinyurl.com/gtnnkak

Books: "Pets and the Afterlife 1, 2 & 3; Lessons Learned from Talking to the Dead; Ghosts and Spirits, Kindred Spirits, Ghosts of England on a Medium's Vacation, Case Files of Inspired Ghost Tracking.

Available in paperback and E-book, on Amazon.com

Another title from Author Rob Gutro:

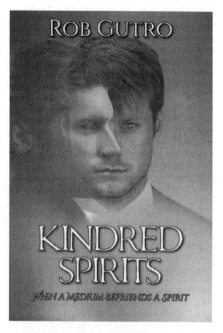

Kindred Spirits: When a Medium Befriends a Spirit
It's uncommon for a medium really get know a spirit so well that the living person considers the spirit a best friend. But that's exactly what happened to medium and paranormal investigator Rob Gutro. When Rob met his partner Tom in 2005, Ed's spirit came along for the ride. Rob never knew Ed in life, but Tom did.

Now, Ed often communicates to Rob and has revealed his sense of humor, his heart, and helped solved the mystery of his passing. Ed's "Spirit Treasure Hunt" showed his family he's with them, too. Ed even sent a look-alike to rescue Rob during a vacation in England. As you read about this special spirit named Ed and his sometimes funny communications, you'll learn signs your loved ones send. This book will teach you how to be more aware of messages from your loved ones in spirit. Available on Amazon.com in paperback and E-book.

Other titles from Author Rob Gutro:

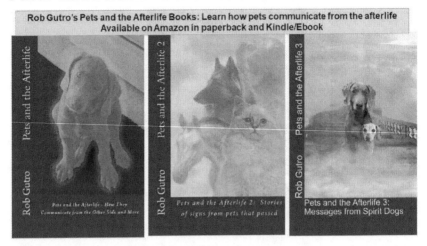

Pets and the Afterlife 1, 2 and 3

The love we share with our pets never dies, and the author proves our pets do communicate with us from the other side. Learn how dogs, cats, horses and some birds have the intelligence and ability to send signs to the living after they pass.

You'll learn when it comes to spirit there is no such thing as a coincidence. Learn how they wait for us when it's our time, what a pet's ashes can do, and the difference between ghosts and spirits. Learn how and why living pets can sense entities. Through personal stories, pet parents relate how their dogs in spirit gave them signs and messages either directly or through a reading with Rob.

These books teach you how to recognize signs and receive messages on your own, and how to work through your grief. Pets 3 includes a special chapter by a licensed professional on how to cope with grief.

Rob's 4 dogs in spirit and spirit dogs from 3 other mediums provided amazing signs. One of Rob's dogs also worked a paranormal investigation and solved a mystery. Available in paperback and E-book on Amazon.com.

Made in United States
Orlando, FL
19 November 2022

24753834R00122